Surplus Military Rifles

Part 1 of 4: United States and Norway

By NRA Technical Staff

MILITARY rifles of the United States have been sold in this country for many years.

Many foreign military rifles and carbines were brought to this country by Servicemen after both World Wars and the Korean War, and a very large number have been imported by arms dealers. Since about 1954, imports of military rifles and ammunition have increased greatly.

All hand-operated rifles are militarily obsolete. Most countries are re-arming with automatic or semi-automatic rifles as rapidly as their means permit, and selling the bolt-action rifles and ammunition being replaced (also a few late-model captured rifles). Arms dealers are purchasing the outmoded rifles and ammunition in large quantities and putting them on the market in this country.

There have been varying views on the intrinsic merits and usefulness of these rifles. Most differences of opinion become less marked when attention is given to qualities of the rifles themselves, and to what the rifles are wanted for. Some of the factors involved, in addition to the very important one of price, are considered below in a general, basic manner.

Safety. Far more time and money can be, and are, devoted to the design, development, and large-scale testing of military rifles than can be spent on any sporting rifle. The severe service to which they are put, and the absolute requirement for success when they are used, make this necessary. Military rifles of the principal nations have the properties of strength and safety to the highest degree that can be attained.

Reliability. The same is true of their reliability, for the same reasons. These rifles are subjected to testing before adoption, and afterward, on a scale unknown for sporting rifles. Their certainty of operation and freedom from parts breakage have reached a level that can be attained in no other way.

Workmanship. Military rifles are the only ones manufactured in very large numbers in single types. They are also the only ones made under the require-ment that their parts must be fully interchangeable, so that repairs can be done by the immediate replacement of parts without hand fitting. They are made with the refinements and exactness of production under these conditions, unlike sporting weapons which must be produced with a limited investment in machinery and gauges.

While the above fundamental factors favor the military rifle, good-quality sporting rifles are entirely adequate in these respects for what they have to do. There are some other factors which also should be considered by the individual who desires a rifle primarily for sporting use.

Finish. Military rifles usually are more roughly finished than sporting rifles. This rule has its exceptions, which in most cases go back to the gradual change in quality of finish given all rifles in recent decades. Before World War I the attention and the skilled work given to finish of both military and sporting rifles were much greater than now, and the quality of finish was

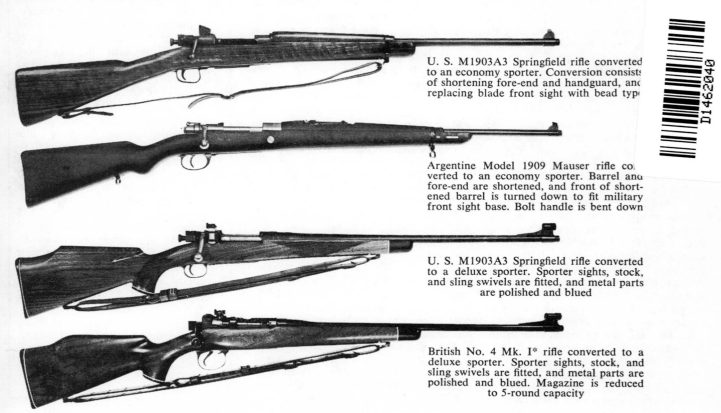

U. S. M1903A3 Springfield rifle converted to an economy sporter. Conversion consists of shortening fore-end and handguard, and replacing blade front sight with bead type

Argentine Model 1909 Mauser rifle converted to an economy sporter. Barrel and fore-end are shortened, and front of shortened barrel is turned down to fit military front sight base. Bolt handle is bent down

U. S. M1903A3 Springfield rifle converted to a deluxe sporter. Sporter sights, stock, and sling swivels are fitted, and metal parts are polished and blued

British No. 4 Mk. I* rifle converted to a deluxe sporter. Sporter sights, stock, and sling swivels are fitted, and metal parts are polished and blued. Magazine is reduced to 5-round capacity

correspondingly higher. Some military rifles of that time were better finished than some present-day sporting rifles. On the other hand, military rifles made late in World War II are extremely rough. This is primarily a matter of appearance, but that can be important in a personal possession.

Condition. Many of the military rifles now on the market are battered and have worn and rusted bores. There is reason to believe that the rifles disposed of so far by some nations are their poorest ones. This condition has seldom been sufficient to make the rifles unserviceable (except in certain types which have generally been advertised as unserviceable), but it does greatly depreciate their value as esteemed possessions.

Type. Some military rifles are of single-shot or other very old types. Others are for very old cartridges or cartridges difficult to obtain on a continuing basis. Such factors can greatly limit or destroy the practical usefulness of a rifle.

Suitability for sporting use. Most buyers desire rifles for hunting game. In military rifles they do obtain powerful, reliable weapons at low cost. However, influenced in various ways, they then often feel impelled to make their rifles resemble sporting rifles, without appreciating that this can lead to expense which defeats the buyer's original purpose. In general, there are 4 situations:

1. Some military rifles can quite practically be used for hunting as they are. At most, replacement of the front sight with a gold or ivory bead may be desirable. A band or ramp is not required and does not improve the rifle; sporting front sights are sold for almost all military rifles to fit on the existing sight base. It is only necessary to select a sight of the correct height, which can be determined by bore-sighting. The rear sights of most military rifles are of much better quality than those of most factory sporting rifles, and the owner should be quite sure of himself before he buys a new rear sight.

2. When military rifles are not suitable as hunting rifles as they are, it is almost always because they are too long and heavy. It is simple to discard handguards and forward bands, shorten the forestock to sporting length, cut off undesired barrel length at the muzzle, and attach a plain front sight band and sight. The owner can do this himself or can have it done at small cost.

3. The rifle can be made over in all its parts except action and barrel. The stock is replaced with one of sporting or heavy target type, sights are likewise replaced, the military trigger replaced with a supposedly better single-

pull type, and the barrel and action polished and reblued. An insufficiently appreciated factor here is cost. All the work except rebluing, but including polishing for rebluing, can be done by the owner. This will keep cost down, though total cost of all the replacement parts should be determined beforehand to avoid later surprises. Provided the owner has taken the time to understand what is required and then does his work well, this can give him great pleasure and a sporting rifle to be proud of. Excellent directions for such work on the Springfield M1903A3, the .303 Lee-Enfield, and the M1 rifles have been published by THE AMERICAN RIFLEMAN and reprints of these are available from the NRA for $1 each. Giving the job to a good gunsmith insures a satisfactory result, but necessarily brings the total cost at least up to that of a medium-grade factory sporting rifle, and with less resale value.

4. All the rifle may be discarded except the action, and a new rifle assembled on that. This is sometimes done with an idea of economy. In reality a rifle action alone is of little or no value for that purpose, and unless the owner can do most of the work himself, including the barrel work, a rifle made up in that way can be expected to cost more than a factory rifle of the same grade. The owner also may intend to use the action for a cartridge quite different from its original one. What is written above concerning the great strength and reliability of military rifles applies to the rifles as made, not altered, and with the ammunition for which they were designed. Putting any rifle action to a use *for which it was not intended*, though it often does turn out well enough because of the extra strength built into the actions, is in most instances a proceeding done in ignorance and is poor practice.

In this and the following 3 issues are given descriptions and data on the principal military rifles, with information on their suitability for conversion to sporting use.

U. S. Model 1898 Krag-Jorgensen Rifle. The Krag-Jorgensen .30-40 rifle, developed by Capt. Ole Krag and Erik Jorgensen of Norway, was the first U. S. Service rifle for smokeless powder and metal-jacketed bullets. It was adopted in 1892, and several models with small improvements were introduced, the most often encountered being the Model 1898.

The Krag is characterized by its smooth-working bolt and horizontal box-magazine with loading gate on right side. It is a well-made and reliable rifle, but its magazine is loaded singly and

U. S. Model 1898 Krag-Jorgensen rifle

U. S. M1903 Springfield rifle

its bolting system is not sufficiently strong for cartridges such as the .30-'06 and .270. In U. S. Krags, only the front locking lug bears on the receiver, and this with incorrect heat-treatment in some bolts results in locking lug breakage.

U. S. Krags were used in the Spanish-American War, Boxer Rebellion, and Philippine Insurrection, and in World War I they were used for guard and training purposes.

This rifle can be easily converted to an excellent sporter by shortening the barrel and fore-end, and fitting a sporting front sight. Carbine versions make a serviceable sporter merely with the replacement of the blade front sight with one of sporting type. Unfortunately, most Krags on the market are not in good condition, and the majority have neglected bores.

Parts are available from dealers, though it is difficult to obtain bolts.

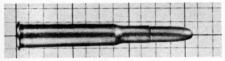

.30-40 KRAG CARTRIDGE
TYPE: Rimmed, bottleneck case
BULLET: 220 grs.
POWDER: Chopped tube smokeless
MUZZLE VELOCITY: 2000 f.p.s.

.30-40 Krag Cartridge. The .30-40 cartridge is also known as the .30 Army or .30 U. S. Army. The "40" in its designation denotes approximately 40 grs. of the smokeless powder used when the cartridge was adopted. The case is rimmed, with considerable body taper and a long neck. The round-nose Service bullet has either a cupronickel-clad steel or cupronickel jacket. There are also some .30-40 Government contract cartridges made between the World Wars which have gilding-metal bullet jackets. Case heads have initials for the manufacturer, and numbers for month and year of production. Many early cartridges made at Frankford Arsenal are tin-plated to prevent chemical reaction of powder on cartridge case.

This cartridge is produced in a variety of sporting loads with various bullet weights by U. S. ammunition manufacturers. Loading components and data are also available. It is an excellent and popular cartridge for deer and similar game. (Cartridges are illustrated on ¼" grid.)

U. S. M1903 Springfield Rifle. The U. S. M1903 rifle, popularly called the Springfield, is a Mauser-type rifle developed at Springfield Armory. The rod bayonet on the first model of this rifle did not find favor with President Theodore Roosevelt, and in 1905 a modified M1903 with knife bayonet and Model 1905 rear sight was introduced. This rifle, modified for the M1906 cartridge, was produced in large quantity at Springfield Armory and Rock Island Arsenal, and was the standard U. S. rifle until adoption of the M1 semi-automatic rifle in 1936.

Principal characteristics of this rifle are its one-piece bolt with 2 forward locking lugs and rear safety lug, and fixed box-magazine which can be loaded singly or with a clip. This rifle is very accurate, and well made, and has a smooth-working reliable action.

Before World War I, M1903 receivers and bolts were made of case-hardened carbon-manganese steel. Some of these rifles suffered burst receivers or broken bolts from high pressure or other abuse. In 1918 a double heat-treatment of the receiver was adopted and this obviated the trouble. This change was made at Springfield Armory with rifle No. 800,000, and at Rock Island about No. 285,507. Receivers earlier than these cannot reliably be improved by any re-heat-treatment.

In World War I the M1903 was one of the principal U. S. rifles, and in World War II it was an extensively used substitute standard arm.

The M1903 is a popular choice for conversion to a sporter. Simple sporterizing involves only shortening of stock and handguard and replacing the front sight with one of sporting type. Many persons find that the buttstock is too short. This can be corrected by replacing the buttplate with a thick recoil pad. The M1903A1 version of this rifle has a well-shaped pistol grip buttstock which will suit the majority of shooters without alteration.

Most specimens of this rifle are in good condition, and many of them are excellent. Parts are available from dealers. This rifle is still sold by several arms dealers, but many specimens are of low-number type which should not be purchased if desired for shooting.

.30-'06 (M2 BALL) CARTRIDGE
TYPE: Rimless, bottleneck case
BULLET: 152 grs.
POWDER: Smokeless, chopped tube or Ball Powder
MUZZLE VELOCITY: 2800 f.p.s.

.30-'06 Cartridge. The .30-'06 cartridge, which was inspired by French and German military spitzer-bullet rounds, was introduced in 1906, and its original loading was a 150-gr. spitzer (pointed) bullet at 2700 f.p.s. muzzle velocity. It was developed from the .30-'03 cartridge which had a case .07" longer than the .30-'06 and a 220-gr. round-nose bullet. In 1925 a .30-'06 M1 cartridge with spitzer boattail bullet was adopted. The M1 cartridge was very accurate and had much greater range than the original Model 1906 load, but it exceeded safety limits of many target ranges then in use. Its long range was found to be of no practical usefulness. Consequently the M1 cartridge was replaced in 1940 by the M2, which has practically the same bullet as the Model 1906 cartridge but 100 f.p.s. higher muzzle velocity.

The M2 ball cartridge has a spitzer flat-base bullet with gilding-metal or gilding-metal-clad steel jacket. This was the standard .30-'06 ball cartridge in World War II and the Korean War. It

U. S. Model 1917 Enfield rifle

U. S. M1903A3 Springfield rifle

U. S. M1 (Garand) rifle

has a crimped-in primer, and is marked with year of production and letters for the manufacturer. Since about 1950 a non-corrosive, non-mercuric primer has been used in this cartridge.

This cartridge is produced in a wide variety of sporting loadings by ammunition manufacturers in this country and several foreign nations. Military cartridges are also available, but only ball or armor-piercing rounds (not tracer or incendiary) should be purchased for shooting. Loading equipment, components, and data are widely available, and the .30-'06 is an excellent choice for target shooting as well as hunting.

```
Specifications
U. S. MODEL 1917 ENFIELD RIFLE
MECHANISM TYPE: Turnbolt; fixed box-magazine
CALIBER: .30-'06
WEIGHT: 9.5 lbs.
BARREL LENGTH: 26.0"
OVER-ALL LENGTH: 46.3"
MAGAZINE CAPACITY: 6 rounds
SIGHTS: Blade front; aperture rear with adjustable
  elevation
RIFLING: 5 grooves, left twist (many specimens rebar-
  reled in World War II have 2 or 4 grooves)
```

U. S. Model 1917 Enfield Rifle. During World War I, U. S. Government armories were unable to produce the Springfield M1903 rifle rapidly enough. The problem was solved by adoption of the Model 1917 Enfield .30-'06 rifle, a slightly modified form of the British Pattern 14 which was ready for manufacture by Winchester, Remington, and Eddystone. These 3 factories produced approximately 2,200,000 Model 1917 rifles.

Except for caliber, this rifle is almost identical to the British Pattern 14 Enfield. The main external differences are that the Model 1917 has no marking disk on buttstock and no long-range auxiliary sights.

The greatest fault of this rifle, and also of the Pattern 14, is rather frequent ejector spring breakage. Other than this, Enfield rifles are noted for their great durability and ruggedness. During World War II U. S. Army

Ordnance developed an improved Enfield ejector spring which overcame the breakage problem.

In addition to their extensive use during World War I, many Model 1917 Enfields were used by this country during World War II, particularly for Reserve Forces and training. The Model 1917 was also used in World War II by the Philippine Army and British Home Guards, and many were used by the Chinese Nationalists against the Communists.

Model 1917 rifles were well made, and those on the market are generally in better condition than British No. 3 Enfields. However, many specimens have neglected bores, and some, especially those made by Eddystone, have cracked receiver rings. These cracks are often not easily detected, and specimens with this fault should not be fired. Parts for this rifle are available from dealers, and simple sporterizing is accomplished by removing handguards and upper and lower bands, and replacing front sight blade with one of sporting type. Often the barrel is shortened to 22" or 24".

```
Specifications
U. S. M1903A3 SPRINGFIELD RIFLE
MECHANISM TYPE: Turnbolt; fixed box-magazine
CALIBER: .30-'06
WEIGHT: 8.6 lbs.
BARREL LENGTH: 24.0"
OVER-ALL LENGTH: 43.2"
MAGAZINE CAPACITY: 5 rounds
SIGHTS: Blade front; aperture rear adjustable for
  windage and elevation
RIFLING: 2 or 4 grooves (a few have 6 grooves), right
  twist
```

U. S. M1903A3 Springfield Rifle. One of the substitute standard U. S. rifles during World War II, the M1903A3 Springfield was produced by Remington Arms Co. and L. C. Smith-Corona, and is similar to the M1903 Springfield but with stamped parts and other manufacturing shortcuts to ease production. An outstanding feature of this rifle is its aperture rear sight on the receiver

bridge, an improvement over the M1903 rear sight which is relatively delicate and too far from the shooter's eye.

Although not very well finished, the M1903A3 is a strong, serviceable rifle. As with the M1903, this rifle can be easily converted to an excellent sporter* by shortening fore-end and handguard, and fitting a sporting front sight.

The M1903A3 is available, and most specimens are in excellent condition. Parts and accessories are also available.

* "Remodeling The 03A3 Springfield", a RIFLEMAN Reprint on converting this rifle to an economy sporter, deluxe sporter, or match rifle is available from the NRA for $1.

```
Specifications
U. S. M1 (GARAND) RIFLE
MECHANISM TYPE: Gas-operated, semi-automatic
CALIBER: .30-'06
WEIGHT: 9.5 lbs.
BARREL LENGTH: 24.0"
OVER-ALL LENGTH: 43.5"
MAGAZINE CAPACITY: 8 rounds
SIGHTS: Blade front; aperture rear adjustable in 1-
  minute clicks for windage and elevation
RIFLING: 4 grooves, right twist
```

U. S. M1 (Garand) Rifle. In the 1920's John Garand, a civilian employee of Springfield Armory, worked intensively on development of a semi-automatic rifle for the U. S. Army, and by the late 20's had worked out a cal. .276 gas-operated rifle with 10-round magazine. This rifle functioned satisfactorily, but the Army Chief of Staff decided against changing the Service rifle caliber to .276. A modified .30-'06 was developed, and after many tests was adopted in 1936. Large-scale production, however, was not begun until 1940. During World War II this rifle was made in large quantity by Winchester as well as Springfield Armory.

The M1 rifle has a simple strong action, well adapted to Service use. It employs a Mannlicher-type clip which is necessary for operation of the arm. The bolt has dual front locking lugs, and is revolved 25° in operation.

In World War II the M1 gave a good

account of itself in both the European and Pacific theaters, and was well liked by troops. After World War II, M1 rifles were used to arm several European NATO nations and Japan and South Korea. The M1 also was used extensively by United Nations Forces in Korea, and in the 1950's some quantities were produced by Harrington & Richardson, Inc., and International Harvester Co. United States production of this famous rifle ceased in May 1957 when the M14 rifle was adopted.

M1 rifles have been converted into sporters by discarding the front handguard and relocating the gas cylinder farther to the rear. This is practicable, but the job requires considerable mechanical skill and a well-equipped shop.

A RIFLEMAN Reprint covering M1 takedown and assembly, conversion to sporter, and accurizing is available from the NRA for 50¢.

Specifications
NORWEGIAN MODEL 1894 KRAG-JORGENSEN RIFLE

MECHANISM TYPE: Turnbolt; fixed box-magazine
CALIBER: 6.5x55 mm.
WEIGHT: 8.8 lbs.
BARREL LENGTH: 30.0"
OVER-ALL LENGTH: 49.7"
MAGAZINE CAPACITY: 5 rounds
SIGHTS: Inverted V front with adjustable windage; open rear with adjustable elevation
RIFLING: 4 grooves, left twist

Norwegian Model 1894 Krag-Jorgensen Rifle. Capt. Ole Krag, a former director of Kongsberg Manufactory in Norway, and Erik Jorgensen, chief armorer of that establishment, were co-developers of the Norwegian Model 1894 Krag-Jorgensen rifle.

6.5X55 CARTRIDGE (ROUND-NOSE BALL)
TYPE: Rimless, bottleneck case
BULLET: 156 grs.
POWDER: Flake smokeless
MUZZLE VELOCITY: 2380 f.p.s.

6.5x55 Cartridge. The 6.5x55 cartridge is adapted to Norwegian Krag-Jorgensen and Swedish Mauser rifles and carbines. "55" in its designation denotes case length in millimeters.

Case head of this cartridge is about 1/100" larger than that of the 8 mm. Mauser and .30-'06, and the extraction cannelure is relatively small. The early 6.5x55 cartridge has a long round-nose bullet, the later form a 139-gr. spitzer-boattail bullet. Norwegian-made cartridges have a rounded primer and are marked RA (Raufoss Ammunition Factory) with month and year of manufacture. Swedish-made cartridges have a flat primer, and are marked with a crown, year of manufacture, and letters K or M to denote Swedish government arsenals. There is also a round-nose type made in Denmark which is marked HA for the Danish arsenal.

Norwegian Model 1912 Krag-Jorgensen Carbine. In 1912 Norway adopted a carbine model of the Krag-Jorgensen, of about the same length as the U. S. M1903 Springfield rifle. This carbine has a medium-length barrel, and its fore-end extends to the muzzle after the fashion of the British Short Magazine Lee-Enfield rifle. The upper band, handguard, and lightweight barrel also show Lee-Enfield influence. Some specimens have a bolt handle with large round knob like that of the Model 1894 Norwegian rifle, but most have a flat bolt handle checkered on both sides.

The Model 1912 carbine was used during the German invasion of Norway in 1940, and also by the Norwegian Home Guard after World War II.

This carbine is well made and finished. Unfortunately, most specimens have neglected bores, and many have cracked or broken stocks. Parts are available from some dealers, and many of the action parts will interchange with those of the Norwegian Model 1894 rifle. Specimens in suitable condition can easily be sporterized by shortening the fore-end and handguard, and fitting a sporting front sight. ■

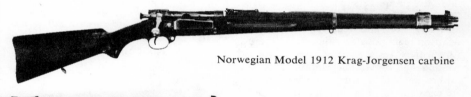

Norwegian Model 1912 Krag-Jorgensen carbine

Norwegian Model 1894 Krag-Jorgensen rifle

The Norwegian Krag is noted for its smooth-working, reliable action. It has a one-piece bolt, with single forward locking lug supplemented by the bolt guide bearing against the receiver bridge. Another principal characteristic is the horizontal box-magazine with loading gate on right side. Unlike most military rifles, the magazine is loaded singly, no clip being provided.

This rifle gave a good account of itself during the German invasion of Norway in World War II.

The excellent workmanship and finish of this rifle, and its smooth-working action and well-proportioned buttstock, are desirable features. Many specimens have neglected bores which make them unsuitable for sporter conversion. For those arms in suitable condition, sporterizing entails shortening barrel and fore-end, fitting a sporting front sight, and possibly shortening the buttstock.

In sporting loadings the 6.5x55 is suitable for deer and similar game. Although not commercially made in this country, it is imported in a variety of sporting and target loadings by Norma-Precision, South Lansing, N. Y. Loading equipment and data are available. U. S. and foreign manufacturers make a wide range of 6.5 mm. bullets, and Norma sells 6.5x55 empty cases adapted to U. S. primers.

Specifications
NORWEGIAN MODEL 1912 KRAG-JORGENSEN CARBINE

MECHANISM TYPE: Turnbolt; fixed box-magazine
CALIBER: 6.5x55 mm.
WEIGHT: 8.8 lbs.
BARREL LENGTH: 24.0"
OVER-ALL LENGTH: 43.6"
MAGAZINE CAPACITY: 5 rounds
SIGHTS: Inverted V front; open rear with adjustable windage and elevation
RIFLING: 4 grooves, left twist

This reprint is from the July 1957, November 1958, May, June, July, August, October, December 1960, January, February 1961 and other issues of THE AMERICAN RIFLEMAN, a fully copyrighted publication.

Surplus Military Rifles

Part 2 of 4: Germany, Argentina, Sweden

By NRA Technical Staff

German Model 1888 Commission rifle

Specifications

GERMAN MODEL 1888 COMMISSION RIFLE

MECHANISM TYPE: Turnbolt; fixed box-magazine
CALIBER: 8 mm. Mauser
WEIGHT: 8.6 lbs.
BARREL LENGTH: 29.1"
OVER-ALL LENGTH: 48.9"
MAGAZINE CAPACITY: 5 rounds
SIGHTS: Inverted V front; open rear adjustable for elevation
RIFLING: 4 grooves, right twist

German Model 1888 Commission Rifle. One of the earliest smokeless powder military rifles was the German Model 1888. It was developed by a German Government Commission, and its design includes Mannlicher's box-magazine and loading clip as well as many bolt and receiver features of Mauser blackpowder rifles. It is therefore often referred to as a Mauser, Mannlicher, or Mauser-Mannlicher rifle.

An unusual feature of this rifle is its sheet metal tube handguard extending from receiver to muzzle (this also appears on the Danish Model 1889 Krag-Jorgensen rifle, and the Belgian Model 1889 Mauser). Other characteristic features are the single-column box-magazine which requires a loading clip for its operation, and the horizontal bolt handle forward of receiver bridge. The horizontal bolt handle is a feature of many foreign military rifles, and is not conducive to fast easy bolt operation, especially from the prone position. The Model 1888 was well made, but not as well designed as Mauser smokeless powder rifles.

Many Model 1888 rifles were used by Germany during World War I, and some by Austria-Hungary. The Austrian designation for this rifle was Repeating Rifle Model 13. The Model 1888 was manufactured by German Government arsenals, and also several firms such as the Austrian Arms Co., Steyr, Austria. This company not only produced this rifle for Germany, but also sold many to China, Brazil, and Peru. Between the World Wars some of this model were also used by Yugoslavia and Ethiopia. Many Chinese specimens differ from the German Model 1888 in that they employ a wood handguard.

This rifle is not well suited for shooting or conversion to a sporter. Workmanship and finish are excellent, but conversion to a nice-appearing sporter is made difficult by the horizontal bolt handle and sheet metal handguard. Also, most specimens on the market are in only fair to poor condition. Parts for this rifle are available from a few dealers.

There is also a carbine version of this weapon with short barrel stocked to the muzzle and a turned-down bolt handle. Carbine specimens in good condition are suitable for sporter use without conversion except that a sporting front sight should be fitted.

**8 MM. MAUSER CARTRIDGE
(MODEL 1888 BALL)**

TYPE: Rimless, bottleneck case
BULLET: 227 grs.
POWDER: Flake smokeless
MUZZLE VELOCITY: 2100 f.p.s.

8 mm. Mauser Cartridge (Model 1888 Ball). This was the first in a series of Mauser rimless smokeless powder cartridges. Although first used in the Model 1888 Commission rifle, it is popularly called 8 mm. Mauser. The long round-nose bullet with cupronickel-clad steel jacket is an important identifying feature. Case head markings show month and year of production, and letters to denote the arsenal or firm and place of manufacture. This cartridge has a smaller diameter bullet and develops less pressure than 8 mm. Mauser spitzer-bullet rounds, and the latter should not be fired in Model 1888 rifles and carbines.

European-made sporting versions of this cartridge are excellent for big-game hunting, and are sold in this country. Imported .318" diameter sporting bullets, U. S.-made cartridge cases, reloading equipment, and loading data for this cartridge are available. Model 1888 clips are sold by dealers. (Cartridges are illustrated on ¼" grid.)

Specifications

GERMAN MODEL 98k MAUSER CARBINE

MECHANISM TYPE: Turnbolt; fixed box-magazine
CALIBER: 8 mm. Mauser
WEIGHT: 8.6 lbs.
BARREL LENGTH: 23.6"
OVER-ALL LENGTH: 43.6"
MAGAZINE CAPACITY: 5 rounds
SIGHTS: Inverted V front; open rear adjustable for elevation
RIFLING: 4 grooves, right twist

German Model 98k Mauser Carbine. In 1935 Germany adopted the Model 98k Mauser carbine for all branches of its armed forces. Development of this weapon was greatly influenced by the experience of World War I.

The Model 98k has the famous turnbolt action developed by Paul Mauser in 1898. Its one-piece bolt has dual forward locking lugs and rear safety lug. The magazine is clip loaded from the top, and can also be loaded singly. This weapon is actually a short rifle of about the same length as the M1903 Springfield, and, unlike many Mausers, has a turned-down bolt handle.

During World War II the 98k was the standard German shoulder arm, and huge quantities were produced in many factories. Specimens made before and during the first part of the war were well made, but quality deteriorated later. Although many wartime specimens are relatively crude, they are safe to fire if in good condition.

Soldiers returning from Europe brought large numbers of the 98k to this country. After the war many of these carbines were acquired by East Germany, Czechoslovakia, Norway, Denmark, Israel, and China. Some saw action with Communist forces in Korea, and many were employed in the 1956 Suez conflict. After Norway adopted the U. S. M1 rifle as standard, they rebarreled their 98k carbines for the .30-'06 cartridge and issued them to the Home Guard.

A well-made 98k in good condition is suitable for conversion to a sporter, but unfortunately many specimens on the market are in fair to poor condition and have the bolt mechanism

German Model 98k Mauser carbine

German Model 98/40 rifle

missing. Model 98 bolts with straight handles are available, but bending the handle down is a job for a gunsmith. Other 98k parts are sold by dealers.

Simple sporterizing of this weapon is accomplished by shortening the fore-end and fitting a sporting front sight. It may be desirable to replace the buttplate with a thick recoil pad to lengthen the stock.

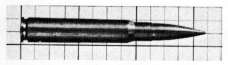

8 MM. MAUSER CARTRIDGE (sS BALL)
TYPE: Rimless, bottleneck case
BULLET: 198 grs.
POWDER: Flake smokeless
MUZZLE VELOCITY: 2476 f.p.s.

8 mm. Mauser Cartridge (sS Ball). There are several 8 mm. Mauser ball cartridges including the Model 1888 with heavy round-nose bullet, the S type with relatively light, pointed bullet, and the sS with spitzer boattail bullet. There is also the S.m.E. (spitzer boattail bullet with iron core) which was used extensively during World War II to conserve lead.

The sS ball cartridge, which was standard for use in the 98k carbine, can be identified by its green primer annulus. Case markings include year of manufacture, lot number, symbol to show case material, and a manufacturer's code. S* denotes a brass case, and St or St⁺ indicates one made of steel. Examples of manufacturer's codes are P101 and aux which are early and late codes, respectively, for the German firm Polte.

8 mm. Mauser sporting cartridges suitable for the 98k and other Mausers are produced in Europe and this country, and are excellent for big-game hunting. Loading data, equipment, and components are readily available. For best results in the 98k and other Mausers with S-type bore, this cartridge should be reloaded with .323″ bullets.

Specifications
GERMAN MODEL 98/40 RIFLE
MECHANISM TYPE: Turnbolt; fixed box-magazine
CALIBER: 8 mm. Mauser
WEIGHT: 8.9 lbs.
BARREL LENGTH: 23.6″
OVER-ALL LENGTH: 43.6″
MAGAZINE CAPACITY: 5 rounds
SIGHTS: Inverted V front; open rear adjustable for elevation
RIFLING: 4 grooves, right twist

German Model 98/40 Rifle. One of the substitute standard weapons used by Germany in World War II was the Model 98/40 rifle. It was produced in Budapest, Hungary, and is a modification of the Model 1935 Hungarian rifle. The 98 in this rifle's designation indicates use of the Model 98 Mauser-type box-magazine and loading clip, and 40 denotes adoption in 1940.

The 98/40 bolt has a separate non-rotating head, and resembles that of German Commission Model 1888 and Mannlicher turnbolt rifles. The buttstock is separate from the fore-end as in the British Lee-Enfield.

This arm is sturdy, and of better quality than many wartime Mausers.

Specifications
GERMAN MODEL 33/40 MAUSER RIFLE
MECHANISM TYPE: Turnbolt; fixed box-magazine
CALIBER: 8 mm. Mauser
WEIGHT: 7.9 lbs.
BARREL LENGTH: 19.3″
OVER-ALL LENGTH: 39.1″
MAGAZINE CAPACITY: 5 cartridges
SIGHTS: Inverted V front; open rear adjustable for elevation
RIFLING: 4 grooves, right twist

German Model 33/40 Mauser Rifle. In 1940 the Germans adopted the Czech Model 1933 Mauser short rifle, slightly modified. This rifle, designated Model 33/40 and adapted to the 8 mm. Mauser cartridge, was produced in Czechoslovakia. It is a short, handy weapon, and was issued mainly to mountain troops.

The 33/40 has a lightened form of the Model 98 Mauser action. Its receiver ring is smaller than that of the 98 Mauser, and the action has several lightening cuts. The action of this rifle is prized by many gunsmiths because of its lightness and fine workmanship, and it is extensively used for building custom sporting rifles.

Many model 33/40 rifles were sold at relatively high prices. Condition of these specimens is excellent to good, but some have neglected bores. Simple sporterizing can be done by shortening fore-end and handguard, and fitting a sporting front sight. Most action parts are interchangeable with those of the Model 98k Mauser, and are available from several dealers.

Specifications
GERMAN MODEL 43 RIFLE
MECHANISM TYPE: Gas-operated, semi-automatic
CALIBER: 8 mm. Mauser
WEIGHT: 9.3 lbs.
BARREL LENGTH: 21.7″
OVER-ALL LENGTH: 44.0″
MAGAZINE CAPACITY: 10 rounds
SIGHTS: Blade front; open rear adjustable for elevation
RIFLING: 4 grooves, right twist

German Model 43 Rifle. The Model 43 rifle, developed by the Walther Arms Co., was the most successful of several German semi-automatic rifles introduced during World War II. It did not replace the bolt-action Mauser, but served principally as a sniping rifle. It has a detachable 4X scope for this purpose, mounted on the right side of the receiver. An advantage of the semi-automatic rifle for sniping is that there is no manual operation of the action to betray the firer's position.

This rifle has a gas mechanism above the barrel like that of the Russian Tokarev rifle, a combination bolt actuator and cover known as the bolt carrier, and a non-rotary bolt with forward dual locking lugs. The detachable magazine can be loaded with two 5-round clips or singly. The design is rather complex and the finish crude. Despite this, functioning is reliable.

Unlike most military rifles, this weapon has a half-length fore-end like that of a sporting rifle, and no provision for attaching a bayonet. Although the fore-end is short, the rifle is fairly heavy because of its laminated beechwood stock.

It is difficult to make a good looking sporter of the Model 43 rifle, and converting it is not recommended.

Specifications
ARGENTINE MODEL 1891 MAUSER RIFLE
MECHANISM TYPE: Turnbolt; detachable box-magazine
CALIBER: 7.65 mm. Mauser
WEIGHT: 8.8 lbs.
BARREL LENGTH: 29.1″
OVER-ALL LENGTH: 48.6″
MAGAZINE CAPACITY: 5 rounds
SIGHTS: Inverted V front; open rear adjustable for elevation
RIFLING: 4 grooves, right twist

Argentine Model 1891 Mauser Rifle. In 1891 Argentina and several other South American nations adopted 7.65 mm. Mauser rifles. Since the

German Model 33/40 Mauser rifle

German Model 43 rifle

Argentine Model 1891 Mauser rifle

Mauser Co. was busily engaged in the 1890's producing rifles for Turkey, most Argentine Model 1891 and other early South American Mausers were made by Ludwig Loewe & Co., Berlin, Germany, and bear the Loewe marking. There are also Argentine Mausers marked to indicate manufacture by the German firm D.W.M. (German Arms and Ammunition Co.). D.W.M., founded in 1896, took over Loewe and also assumed financial control of the Mauser Co.

This rifle is well made and durable, but lacks several desirable features of later Mausers. It has the characteristic Mauser one-piece bolt with dual forward locking lugs, but has no safety lug. Cocking occurs while closing the bolt. The magazine is of single-column type which projects beneath the stock. It can be loaded with a clip or singly. In compliance with Argentine law, exported specimens have the Argentine coat of arms ground off the receiver ring.

Issued and simply sporterized rifles are available from surplus arms dealers at low prices. While condition of most specimens ranges from perfect to excellent (except for ground-off coat of arms), this rifle is not as desirable as later Mausers in action design. Simple sporterizing is accomplished by shortening barrel and fore-end, fitting a sporting front sight, and bending down the bolt handle. The latter job should be done by a competent gunsmith.

**7.65 MM. MAUSER CARTRIDGE
(ROUND-NOSE BALL)**

TYPE: Rimless, bottle-neck case
BULLET: 211 grs.
POWDER: Flake smokeless
MUZZLE VELOCITY: 2132 f.p.s.

7.65 mm. Mauser Cartridge (Round-nose Ball). The early 7.65 mm. Mauser cartridge for the Argentine Model 1891 Mauser has a long round-nose bullet with cupronickel-clad steel jacket. Except for its short case neck, it is similar in appearance to the 8 mm. Mauser Model 1888 cartridge. Markings on a typical specimen made under contract in Germany include year of production, "D.M." for German Ammunition Co., and "K." for Karlsruhe, where this firm was located.

The later spitzer and spitzer boattail 7.65 mm. Mauser cartridges can also be fired in Argentine Model 1891 rifles, but the long cylindrical bullet seat in the Model 1891 barrel is not well adapted to pointed bullets.

Sporting and military versions of this cartridge were produced in this country for many years, but have been discontinued. The sporting version is excellent for big-game hunting.

Cartridge cases can be made from .30-'06 cases, using forming dies available from loading tool manufacturers, and .311"-.312" diameter .303 British bullets available from several manufacturers are the correct size for this cartridge. Loading data and equipment are available. Argentine military ammunition has Berdan primers, but can be reloaded using a Berdan primer decapping tool and European-made 5.5 mm. primers which are available in this country.

Argentine Model 1909 Mauser Rifle. The Argentine Model 1909 rifle is one of the many Mausers based on the German Model 1898, to which it is generally similar in design and appearance. Some distinctive features of this arm are the hinged magazine floorplate with release in trigger guard, and the peculiar auxiliary bayonet lug for the Model 1891 Argentine bayonet.

Most specimens sold in this country were made in Germany by D.W.M., but some are not marked as to manufacturer. In accordance with Argentine law, the Argentine coat of arms was ground off the receiver before sale.

This rifle shows fine workmanship and finish, and most specimens are in good to perfect condition (except for ground-off coat of arms). It is very desirable for conversion to a sporter, and simple sporterizing is done by shortening barrel and fore-end, fitting a sporting front sight, and bending down the bolt handle.

**7.65 MM. MAUSER CARTRIDGE
(SPITZER BOATTAIL BALL)**
TYPE: Rimless, bottleneck case
BULLET: 185 grs.
POWDER: Flake smokeless
MUZZLE VELOCITY: 2467 f.p.s.

7.65 mm. Mauser Cartridge (Spitzer Boattail Ball). Modern 7.65 mm. Mauser ball cartridges have either a relatively light spitzer bullet or a heavy spitzer bullet with boattail. The latter is the most modern type adapted to the Argentine Model 1909 Mauser, and was produced in Argentine factories. It has a green primer annulus for identification. This cartridge gives excellent performance.

This cartridge can be reloaded with U. S.-made powder and .311″-.312″ diameter bullets, and loading data and equipment are available. Primers are of Berdan type, and European 5.5 mm. Berdan primers are available. Cases can be made from .30-'06 cartridge cases, and forming dies are available.

Swedish Model 1896 Mauser Rifle. In 1896 Sweden adopted a 6.5x55 Mauser rifle. It closely resembles the Model 1893 Spanish Mauser, but has a guide rib on the bolt and a deep cut in left receiver wall to facilitate magazine loading. It also has an upward projection on the cocking piece which permits the firing pin to be eased forward with the thumb. It cocks on the closing bolt motion.

This rifle was produced by the Carl Gustafs Stads Rifle Factory, the Husqvarna Arms Co. in Sweden, and by the Mauser Co. in Germany. Finland used this rifle extensively in the 1939-40 Russo-Finnish War, and a quantity were purchased and used by Denmark after World War II. There is also a Swedish Model 1938 short rifle and a Model 1894 carbine. These have the same action as the Model 1896 rifle, and are adapted to the 6.5x55 cartridge.

The high-quality workmanship and finish of this rifle are very desirable, but unfortunately most specimens on the market have neglected bores. Specimens in good condition can be sporterized by shortening barrel and fore-end, fitting a sporting front sight, and bending down the bolt handle. The carbine has a short barrel stocked to muzzle and turned-down bolt handle, and requires only a sporting front sight to make it into a suitable sporter. Action parts for rifle and carbine are interchangeable and available. ∎

A MAN TO REMEMBER

JOHN C. GARAND
Invented the Garand rifle

*Born—Jan. 1888,
St. Remi, Quebec,
Canada*

JOHN GARAND spent only 10 years in Canada before his parents moved to Denisonville, Conn., and then on to Jewett City. At age 20 he became a tool- and gauge-maker for Browne & Sharpe and then in 1914 he became acting foreman and machine designer for Federal Screw Corp. in Providence, R. I.

From Providence, Garand moved to New York City, and it was there that he turned his attention to developing automatic firearms. The first World War focused attention on such weapons, and Garand was interested to learn of the frequent malfunctions that plagued them.

Having conceived some designs which he thought would eliminate such failures, he approached the Naval Invention Bureau and was soon put to work at the National Bureau of Standards in Washington, where he successfully developed a primer-activated light machine gun. There Maj. Lee Wright met the inventor and was sufficiently impressed to obtain Army Ordnance sponsorship and move Garand to the Springfield Armory in 1919.

Garand's machine gun had been soundly designed, but it failed to perform the functions the Army desired in such an arm. Thus Garand was instructed to develop a semiautomatic rifle, and this he proceeded to do, still using the explosion of the primer to activate the mechanism. He succeeded in perfecting such an arm only to have a change in ammunition adopted in 1925 force him to redesign his rifle, this time utilizing gas pressure for the activation.

Tests of the new rifle were highly satisfactory, but before even limited production could be started the caliber of the rifle was ordered increased from .276 to .30, and this caused further delays and alterations before the final adoption of the arm on Jan. 9, 1936. Garand is retired and lives in Springfield, Mass.—HAROLD L. PETERSON

Argentine Model 1909 Mauser rifle

Swedish Model 1896 Mauser rifle

Surplus Military Rifles

Part 3 of 4: Great Britain, Switzerland, Russia

By NRA Technical Staff

British No. 1 Mk. III* Lee-Enfield rifle

British No. 1 Mk. III* Lee-Enfield Rifle. Commonly called the .303 Lee-Enfield, this rifle was adapted from the design of an American, James P. Lee, and produced in the Royal Small Arms Factory at Enfield, England. It is also known as the SMLE (Short Magazine Lee-Enfield). Mk. III denotes the third form of the No. 1 rifle, and the asterisk indicates a modification of this version. In addition, large quantities of this rifle were produced in England by the BSA Co., and in Australia and India.

One of the chief characteristics of this rifle is its smooth-working action. Its rear-positioned locking lugs give a short bolt turn and throw, and make this one of the fastest turnbolt rifles to operate. The magazine is loaded with two 5-round clips or singly. Although the unconventional lines of this rifle, particularly the low-comb stock, do not find general favor, the Lee-Enfield is well-made and reliable, and one of the best military turnbolt rifles.

This rifle was used in both World Wars. Before World War I it was criticized because of certain design features, but it proved itself to be a splendid military arm and was well liked by British troops.

This rifle has excellent workmanship and a smooth-working action which are highly desirable. However, many specimens are considerably worn and have neglected bores which make them unsuitable for sporter conversion. Simple sporterizing of specimens in suitable condition consists of shortening the fore-end, discarding handguards, nose-cap, and lower band, and fitting a sporting front sight.

.303 BRITISH CARTRIDGE (MK. VII BALL)
TYPE: Rimmed, bottleneck case
BULLET: 174 grs.
POWDER: Tubular cordite or chopped-tube nitrocellulose smokeless
MUZZLE VELOCITY: 2440 f.p.s.

.303 British Cartridge. There are many marks or models of .303 British ball cartridges, the most common being the Mk. VII which was introduced in 1910 and used in both World Wars. The Mk. VII has a spitzer, flat-base bullet with cupronickel jacket. The bullet has an aluminum or fiber filler in the forward part of the jacket to give the desired length without excessive weight.

Case headstamp includes the Roman numeral VII, date of production, and initials for place of manufacture. Cartridges loaded with nitrocellulose powder are usually marked VII Z.

Sporting cartridges in this caliber are produced commercially in this country and several others, and are excellent for big-game shooting. Loading equipment, components, and data are readily obtainable for U. S.-made .303 British cartridges. British-made cartridges have a special large-size Berdan primer with mercuric composition which makes them unsuitable for reloading. (Cartridges are illustrated on ¼" grid.)

British No. 3 Mk. I* Enfield Rifle. This rifle, popularly known by its earlier designation Pattern 14, was adopted in 1914. It was changed in caliber from a Mauser-type cal. .276 rifle which the British experimented with shortly before World War I.

The one-piece bolt of this rifle and magazine with staggered cartridge column are typical Mauser features. Cocking is on the closing bolt motion, as in earlier smokeless-powder Mausers. However, the rotary safety on right side of receiver is of British origin. The bolt handle has a peculiar rearward bend to clear the rear sight on the receiver bridge. In addition to the regular sights, this rifle has long-range auxiliary sights consisting of an aperture on left side of receiver and a bead front sight on an arm pivoted to left side of fore-end.

During World War I this rifle was produced in small numbers in this country by Winchester, Remington in Ilion, N. Y., and a Remington-owned plant at Eddystone, Pa. The British Army employed this rifle with a telescope sight for sniping in that war, and the Royal Navy also used it. During World War II it was a substitute standard rifle.

This rifle was well made, but specimens now sold by dealers usually are in only fair condition and have neglected bores. Simple sporterizing is accomplished by removing handguards and upper and lower bands, and replacing front sight blade with one of sporting type. Many persons shorten the barrel to 22" or 24".

British No. 4 Mk. I Rifle. The No. 4 rifle was developed from the No. 1 SMLE between the World Wars. It retained the basic Lee action design of the No. 1 rifle, but was extensively modified to improve performance and ease manufacture. The more important modifications included a heavier barrel, heavier receiver, aperture rear sight, and simplified bedding of barrel in fore-end.

Few No. 4 rifles were made until after the Battle of Dunkirk. After that battle it was produced in huge quantities in England, Canada, and the United States, and was one of the principal British Service rifles in World War II. Many wartime-produced No. 4 rifles are a slightly modified form designated No. 4 Mk. I*. Following World War II many No. 4 rifles were used by Italy, Greece, and the Arab States. In 1954 the No. 4 was replaced in the British, Australian, and Canadian Services by the FN semi-automatic rifle chambered for the 7.62 NATO cartridge.

No. 4 rifles are usually in better condition than the average No. 1 SMLE. However, the finish of most No. 4 rifles is far rougher than peacetime standard, and this is a factor to consider in suitability for sporter conversion* even though the arm is safe and serviceable. Parts for this rifle are available.

*The RIFLEMAN Reprint "Remodeling the .303 Lee-Enfield Rifle" gives detailed historical and technical information on these arms, .303 British cartridge loading data, and instructions for deluxe sporterizing. Price, 50¢ from NRA Headquarters.

```
............................................
          Specifications
     BRITISH NO. 5 MK. I RIFLE
MECHANISM TYPE: Turnbolt; detachable box-magazine
CALIBER: .303 British
WEIGHT: 7.2 lbs.
BARREL LENGTH: 20.5" (w/flash hider)
OVER-ALL LENGTH: 39.1"
MAGAZINE CAPACITY: 10 rounds
SIGHTS: Blade front; aperture rear adjustable for
    elevation
RIFLING: 5 grooves, left twist
............................................
```

British No. 5 Mk. I Rifle. During World War II the British No. 1 SMLE and No. 4 rifles were found to be too long and heavy for jungle fighting, and a shorter rifle designated No. 5 Mk. I was developed and adopted. This weapon, known popularly as the 'jungle carbine', is essentially a modified No. 4 rifle with short fore-end and barrel, and fitted with a flash hider and rubber buttplate. The short fore-end gives this arm the appearance of a sporting rifle.

Many of these rifles were produced. They were used principally in Burma and the Pacific islands during the latter part of World War II.

This rifle is popular with shooters because of its handiness and sporting rifle appearance. It is suitable for a sporter as is, except that most shooters replace the military blade front sight with one of sporting type and some, finding the buttstock too short, fit a thick recoil pad. Parts for this rifle are available from arms dealers.

```
............................................
          Specifications
  SWISS MODEL 1889 SCHMIDT-RUBIN RIFLE
MECHANISM TYPE: Straight-pull bolt; detachable box-
    magazine
CALIBER: 7.5 mm.
WEIGHT: 10.3 lbs.
BARREL LENGTH: 30.7"
OVER-ALL LENGTH: 51.2"
MAGAZINE CAPACITY: 12 rounds
SIGHTS: Inverted V front; open rear adjustable for
    elevation
RIFLING: 3 grooves, right twist
............................................
```

Swiss Model 1889 Schmidt-Rubin Rifle. In 1889 Switzerland adopted a straight-pull rifle developed by Col. Rudolf Schmidt, Director of the Federal Armory in Bern. Col. Eduard Rubin, Director of the Federal Ammunition Factory in Thun, developed the 7.5 mm. cartridge for this arm.

The Model 1889 straight-pull action has a ring on the cocking piece for manual cocking and putting the arm on safe. Dual locking lugs are on a sleeve which is revolved by cam engagement with an action rod. Locking shoulders in the receiver are behind the magazine. Magazine loading is with two 6-round clips or singly. While very well made and finished, the 1889 is a heavy, unwieldy rifle, and has an undesirably long action.

Due to its long action and protruding magazine, this rifle is not well suited for conversion to a sporter.

7.5 mm. Swiss Cartridge (Model 90/03 Ball). There are several models of 7.5 mm. ball cartridge adapted to the

Model 1889 rifle, and the Model 90/03 has been chosen as representative. The rimless case is of slightly larger head diameter than the .30-'06 and Mauser rimless cartridges, and the case shoulder is rather abrupt. The 90/03 bullet is lead alloy with lubricated paper-patch on its bearing surface and a cupro-nickel-clad steel jacket over the nose to gain penetration. Headstamp markings include numerals for month and year of production, and letters (left letter shows where case was produced, and right letter where loaded). This round has a flat primer with black annulus. There is also a Model 90 cartridge adapted to the Model 1889 rifle which has a rounded primer.

7.5 MM. SWISS CARTRIDGE
(MODEL 90/03 BALL)
TYPE: Rimless, bottleneck case
BULLET: 211 grs.
POWDER: Smokeless
MUZZLE VELOCITY: 1980 f.p.s.

This cartridge is Berdan-primed and not produced in this country. There is also a Model 90/23 cartridge with metal-jacketed round-nose bullet which is adapted to the Model 1889 rifle. Loading data for these cartridges are not available.

```
............................................
          Specifications
       SWISS MODEL 1911 RIFLE
MECHANISM TYPE: Straight-pull bolt; detachable box-
    magazine
CALIBER: 7.5 mm.
WEIGHT: 10.2 lbs.
BARREL LENGTH: 30.7"
OVER-ALL LENGTH: 51.6"
MAGAZINE CAPACITY: 6 rounds
SIGHTS: Blade front; open rear adjustable for elevation
RIFLING: 4 grooves, right twist
............................................
```

Swiss Model 1911 Rifle. The Swiss Model 1911 rifle is basically like the Model 1889 Schmidt-Rubin, but has a 6-round magazine, pistol-grip stock, and 4-groove barrel dimensioned for the Model 1911 cartridge. The action of this rifle is slightly shorter than that of the Model 1889, and its locking lugs are on the forward part of the bolt sleeve. There is also a carbine version of the Model 1911 with 23.3" barrel.

British No. 3 Mk. I* Enfield rifle

British No. 4 Mk. I rifle

British No. 5 Mk. I rifle

Swiss Model 1889 Schmidt-Rubin rifle

Swiss Model 1911 rifle

Russian Model 1891/30 Mosin-Nagant rifle

Russian Model 1940 Tokarev rifle

Like the Swiss Model 1889, this rifle is not suitable for conversion to a sporter because of its long action. The Model 1911 carbine is much shorter than the rifle, and makes a fair hunting weapon as issued.

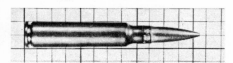

7.5 MM. SWISS CARTRIDGE
(MODEL 1911 BALL)

TYPE: Rimless, bottleneck case
BULLET: 174 grs.
POWDER: Flake smokeless
MUZZLE VELOCITY: 2640 f.p.s.

7.5 mm. Swiss Cartridge (Model 1911 Ball). The Model 1911 Swiss cartridge is adapted to Swiss Model 1911 rifles and carbines and the Model 1931 short rifle. It develops considerably more pressure than the 90/03 and other early 7.5 mm. cartridges with round-nose bullet, and should not be fired in Schmidt-Rubin Model 1889 rifles. It has a spitzer boattail bullet with cupronickel-clad steel jacket, and junction of case mouth and bullet is sealed with a wax-like lubricant. Propellant is progressive-burning flake nitrocellulose. The system of headstamp marking is like that of the Swiss Model 90/03 cartridge. The Model 1911 cartridge is a modern, well-designed round with excellent ballistic performance.

This cartridge is available from a few arms dealers, but it has a mercuric primer and should not be reloaded.

Specifications
RUSSIAN MODEL 1891/30 MOSIN-NAGANT
RIFLE

MECHANISM TYPE: Turnbolt; fixed box-magazine
CALIBER: 7.62 mm. Russian
WEIGHT: 8.6 lbs.
BARREL LENGTH: 28.7"
OVER-ALL LENGTH: 48.4"
MAGAZINE CAPACITY: 5 rounds
SIGHTS: Post front; open rear adjustable for elevation
RIFLING: 4 grooves, right twist

Russian Model 1891/30 Mosin-Nagant Rifle. The Model 1891/30 rifle was adopted in 1930, and is an im-

proved form of the Russian Model 1891 rifle developed by the Russian Col. S. I. Mosin and the Belgian arms designer Nagant. It is popularly known as the Mosin or Mosin-Nagant rifle.

The bolt head of this rifle has dual locking lugs, and is fastened to the bolt by a connector bar. The bolt handle is forward of the receiver bridge, and serves as a safety lug. The single-column magazine extends beneath the stock, and can be loaded with a clip or singly. An interrupter separates the upper round in the magazine from those beneath to prevent jams during feeding of the rimmed cartridges. Although strong and serviceable in its original caliber, the Mosin is rather awkward to operate and does not have a smooth working action.

From 1930 until about 1950 the Model 1891/30 was the standard Soviet rifle, and currently is substitute standard. It is used in large numbers by Communist satellite nations. This rifle served the Russians well in World War II, and was also employed extensively by Communist forces in Korea.

Because it does not have a smooth-working action and the finish on most specimens leaves much to be desired, this rifle is not particularly suited for sporter conversion.

Russian Model 1940 Tokarev Rifle. The Model 1940 7.62 mm. Tokarev was the principal Russian semi-automatic rifle during World War II. It was developed by the Russian arms designer, Tokarev, who also designed a Russian Service pistol. This rifle was extensively employed during the war, especially for sniping, but it did not replace hand-operated Mosin-Nagant rifles and carbines.

Principal characteristics of the Tokarev rifle are its gas mechanism above the barrel, bolt carrier which covers and actuates the bolt, and detachable box-magazine which can be loaded with two 5-round clips or singly. The bolt is of simple design, and locks

```
Specifications
RUSSIAN MODEL 1940 TOKAREV RIFLE
MECHANISM TYPE: Gas-operated, semi-automatic
CALIBER: 7.62 mm.
WEIGHT: 8.6 lbs.
BARREL LENGTH: 24.6"
OVER-ALL LENGTH: 48.1"
MAGAZINE CAPACITY: 10 rounds
SIGHTS: Post front: open rear adjustable for elevation
RIFLING: 4 grooves, right twist
```

against a shoulder on the receiver behind the magazine. The Tokarev is well designed, but the 7.62 mm. rimmed cartridge frequently causes feeding difficulties. When employed as a sniping rifle, the Tokarev was fitted with a compact 3X scope sight.

Some of these rifles are of selective-fire type, and the safety lock serves as the selector lever. Selective-fire specimens, quite rare and identified by clearance cuts in the bottom of the stock on both sides of the safety, come under provisions of the National Firearms Act, and must be registered with the Alcohol and Tobacco Tax Division, U. S. Treasury Dept.

Converting the Tokarev to a sporter is not recommended. Many specimens have the magazine missing. Tokarev magazines are hard to find and expensive, but are occasionally available.

7.62 MM. RUSSIAN CARTRIDGE (M1908 BALL)

TYPE: Rimmed, bottleneck case
BULLET: 150 grs.
POWDER: Chopped tube smokeless
MUZZLE VELOCITY: 2850 f.p.s.

7.62 mm. Russian Cartridge. The 7.62 mm. Russian cartridge for the Mosin-Nagant and Tokarev rifles is rimmed, and designated M1908 ball or light pointed ball. It has a large-diameter case body, and outer edge of case head is beveled. The primer is flat, and larger than in most military cartridges. The cartridge case is brass- or copper-plated steel, and marked with year of production and a number code for the manufacturer.

This cartridge was produced in this country for many years, but has been discontinued. It can be reloaded with cal. .30 bullets, and loading data and equipment are available.

U. S.-produced cartridges in this caliber are adapted to the large diameter American rifle primer, but Russian-produced cartridges require a Berdan primer not available in this country. ∎

A MAN TO REMEMBER

FERDINAND RITTER VON MANNLICHER

Developed over 150 models of automatic and repeating firearms

Born—Mainz, Germany, 1848
Died—Austria, 1904

FERDINAND Ritter von Mannlicher was a staunch Austrian patriot who seemed to view all of his inventions and developments in the light of their service to his country. Little is known of his personal life, which he kept subordinated to his driving interest in and genius for the mechanics of firearms. It is hard to appreciate the scope of his experiments and developments in this field. In his work he anticipated many of the basic features in use today, and made some contribution to most systems then in use.

Perhaps the best known of his developments was the packet, or clip, system of magazine loading. A start had been made in packet loading with the loading tubes for the Spencer rifle, which some soldiers carried in their quick-loader boxes during the Civil War, but von Mannlicher brought forth the clip as it is known today, the first really successful and widely used device of the sort. The clip of the modern Garand rifle is only a modification of von Mannlicher's original design.

In 1880, at the age of 32, von Mannlicher brought out a repeating rifle with a turning-bolt action. In 1884 he developed the first of several straight-pull magazine rifles for which he is famous. In 1885 came his first fully automatic weapon, a light machine gun which foreshadowed many modern types but was far ahead of its time and was impractical. The year 1887 saw the bolt-action rifle having a magazine with revolving spool-shaped cartridge follower of the type used in Austrian Mannlicher-Schoenauer and American Savage and Johnson high-powered rifles today. In 1891 he introduced a clip-loading semi-automatic rifle and another in 1893, and then came automatic pistols with both locked breech and delayed-blowback systems, far ahead of their time but foreshadowing developments to come.—HAROLD L. PETERSON

A MAN TO REMEMBER

PETER PAUL MAUSER
Developed the Mauser rifles

Born—Oberndorf, Württemberg, June 27, 1838
Died—May 1914

PAUL MAUSER, as he was usually called, was born into a gunmaking family. His father was a master gunsmith in the royal firearms factory at Oberndorf, and 6 of his older brothers also learned the trade. By the time he was 12 and before he graduated from school he was already working part time. In 1852 he joined his father and brothers in the government factory, where he quickly attracted attention for his ability to develop new methods which speeded production.

After a brief tour of duty in the Army in 1859, Mauser began the developmental work which brought him fame. Teaming up with his older brother Wilhelm, he first produced a breech-loading cannon and projectile. While interesting and functional, it was never adopted. He next turned his attention to small arms and set out to improve the bolt action originated by Dreyse for the needle gun. He succeeded and produced an action that would cock while opening and closing the bolt. There followed several years of unsuccessful efforts to market the new rifle, which included a contract with the American Samuel Norris and work at Liege, Belgium, as Mauser further perfected his gun. Finally, in 1871 Prussia adopted the Mauser rifle and production began in 1872. The first Mauser plant was destroyed by fire in 1873, but substantial orders for arms from Prussia and Württemberg enabled the brothers to buy the royal arms factory at Oberndorf and begin operation there in 1874. Other orders were obtained from China and Serbia, assuring the new company of success and permitting Paul Mauser to devote his primary energy to the development of repeating rifles, revolvers, automatics, and the long line of arms that bear his name. He was active until his death at 76.— HAROLD L. PETERSON.

Surplus Military Rifles

By NRA Technical Staff

Japanese Model 38 Arisaka rifle

Japanese Model 99 rifle

> **Specifications**
> **JAPANESE MODEL 38 ARISAKA RIFLE**
> MECHANISM TYPE: Turnbolt; fixed box-magazine
> CALIBER: 6.5 mm. Arisaka
> WEIGHT: 9.2 lbs.
> BARREL LENGTH: 31.4"
> OVER-ALL LENGTH: 50.2"
> MAGAZINE CAPACITY: 5 rounds
> SIGHTS: Inverted V front; open rear adjustable for elevation
> RIFLING: 6 grooves, right twist

Japanese Model 38 Arisaka Rifle. The Japanese Model 38 rifle was approved in 1905 (38th year of Emperor Meiji's reign) and adopted in 1906. It is a Mauser-type rifle developed by Col. Nariaki Arisaka, Superintendent of Tokyo Arsenal.

This rifle has a rotary knob safety, mainspring inside the firing pin, and sheet-metal breech cover. Its action is strong and reliable, and the rifle is well made from good materials. Markings on the receiver include the Imperial chrysanthemum, and model designation in Japanese characters. Many specimens brought to this country by soldiers during the World War II period have the chrysanthemum ground off.

This weapon should not be confused with cheaply-made 6.5 mm. Japanese training rifles which are smoothbored, and adapted only to blank cartridges. These training rifles usually have cast or forged receivers with integral tangs, and rarely bear Japanese Imperial seal or usual model designations.

The Model 38 was standard in the Japanese Service from 1906 to World War II. It was also used for training by the British during World War I, and the Communists employed some of these rifles during the Korean Conflict.

This rifle is quite popular for conversion to a sporter, and when properly converted is a good deer rifle. The conversion job consists of shortening barrel and fore-end, fitting a sporting front sight, and bending down the bolt handle. The Model 38 does not find favor with some shooters because its action does not work as smoothly as several other bolt-action rifles.

6.5 MM. ARISAKA CARTRIDGE (SPITZER BALL)
TYPE: Semi-rimmed, bottleneck case
BULLET: 139 grs.
POWDER: Flake smokeless
MUZZLE VELOCITY: 2500 f.p.s.

6.5 mm. Arisaka Cartridge. Ball cartridges of this caliber include the early type with round-nose bullet, and the later type with 139-gr. spitzer bullet that was standard in the Japanese army during World War II.

This cartridge is of semi-rimmed type, and the case capacity is relatively small. The case bears no headstamp, and the primer is rounded. The bullet usually has a red band at the junction with case mouth. An unusual feature is that the spitzer bullet has a much thicker jacket at the forward part than at the rear. As with the aluminum tip in the British Mk. VII bullet, this gives a long bullet for its weight.

A special Berdan primer is required for the Japanese military cartridge, and this precludes reloading. However, commercial loadings of this cartridge with soft-point bullets are available from Norma, and these can be reloaded with American primers. The sporting cartridge is good for deer hunting, and loading data, equipment, and components are available. (Cartridges are illustrated on ¼" grid.)

> **Specifications**
> **JAPANESE MODEL 99 RIFLE**
> MECHANISM TYPE: Turnbolt; fixed box-magazine
> CALIBER: 7.7 mm.
> WEIGHT: 8.0 lbs.
> BARREL LENGTH: 25.8"
> OVER-ALL LENGTH: 43.9"
> MAGAZINE CAPACITY: 5 rounds
> SIGHTS: Inverted V front; aperture rear adjustable for elevation
> RIFLING: 4 grooves, right twist

Japanese Model 99 Rifle. In 1939 (Japanese year 2599) Japan adopted the Model 99 rifle. This rifle is considerably shorter than the Japanese Model 38 Arisaka rifle, and adapted to a 7.7 rimless cartridge. There is also a Model 99 long rifle, but relatively few were produced. Except for small modifications to ease manufacture, the Model 99 action is like that of the Model 38 rifle.

Unusual features of this arm are the sighting bars pivoted to rear sight leaf for taking leads on aircraft, and the wire monopod fastened to lower band. Many specimens made late in World War II lack these features.

The Model 99 was used in large numbers during World War II. It is a serviceable rifle, but not as well made as the Model 38 Arisaka. Specimens made during latter part of World War II are crude.

Many Model 99 rifles have been converted to .30-'06 in this country by simply reaming the chamber. This practice is not recommended as the 7.7 mm. chamber is too large at the rear for .30-'06, and there is excessive expansion of the cartridge case.

Because it is relatively crude, this rifle is not as suitable for conversion to a sporter as the Japanese Model 38. It is reasonably light and compact, and fairly well adapted for hunting without conversion.

7.7 MM. CARTRIDGE (BALL)
TYPE: Rimless, bottleneck case
BULLET: 183 grs.
POWDER: Chopped tube smokeless
MUZZLE VELOCITY: 2300 f.p.s.

7.7 mm. Rimless Cartridge. In addition to its use in the Model 99 rifle, the 7.7 mm. rimless cartridge is adapted to the Japanese Model 99 light machine gun and is often confused with the 7.7 mm. semi-rimmed heavy machine gun cartridge which it closely resembles. Like the Japanese 6.5 mm. spitzer ball cartridge, the pointed bullet of this round has an extra thick jacket forward which makes the bullet long for its weight. The primer is flat and secured in the case by an annular crimp. The case head is unmarked, and the bullet is encircled by a red band where it meets the case mouth.

This cartridge is difficult to get in its original military loading, but it is readily available from Norma in sporting loads with various bullet weights. It is an excellent big-game cartridge similar in performance to the .30-40 Krag, .303 British, and 8 mm. Mauser. As made by Norma, it is adapted to large-size American rifle primers. The .311"-.312" diameter .303 British bullets are correct for this cartridge. Equipment, data, and components for reloading this cartridge are available.

Italian Model 1891 Carcano rifle

Specifications
ITALIAN MODEL 1891 CARCANO RIFLE
MECHANISM TYPE: Turnbolt; fixed box-magazine
CALIBER: 6.5 mm. Carcano
WEIGHT: 8.4 lbs.
BARREL LENGTH: 30.8"
OVER-ALL LENGTH: 50.5"
MAGAZINE CAPACITY: 6 rounds
SIGHTS: Inverted V front; open rear adjustable for elevation
RIFLING: 4 grooves, right twist with increasing pitch toward muzzle

Italian Model 1891 Carcano Rifle. The Italian Model 1891 Service rifle, popularly known as the Carcano, was developed by Col. Parravicino, factory director, and M. Carcano, chief inspector, of the Turin Arms Factory. It is also called the Parravicino-Carcano, Mannlicher-Carcano, or Terni rifle. The name Mannlicher has reference to its Mannlicher-type magazine and cartridge clip, and Terni is the city in Italy where many of these rifles were produced.

The Carcano has a one-piece bolt with dual forward locking lugs, and the bolt handle is forward of the receiver bridge. Its single-column Mannlicher-type magazine cannot be used without a cartridge clip. There have been stories that the small lug on its bolt sleeve is

liable to break and allow the firing mechanism to be driven rearward. However, when the bolt is closed the firing mechanism is securely retained by a large lug on the bolt sleeve engaging a receiver shoulder. Although not well finished, the Carcano is a sturdy rifle, and safe to fire if in good condition.

Italy used this rifle in both World Wars, and some were also employed by Yugoslavia and Albania.

The crude finish and appearance of this rifle make it a poor choice for conversion to a sporter.

6.5 MM. CARCANO CARTRIDGE (BALL)
TYPE: Rimless, bottleneck case
BULLET: 162 grs.
POWDER: Chopped tube smokeless
MUZZLE VELOCITY: 2296 f.p.s.

6.5 mm. Carcano Cartridge. The 6.5 mm. Carcano cartridge is not interchangeable with other 6.5 mm. rounds. Its principal identifying features are a long bullet with slightly blunted point, and the groove on case head encircling the primer. The bullet jacket is either gilding-metal-clad steel or cupronickel, and there usually are stab crimps around the case neck. The cartridge case is either brass or steel.

This cartridge and the 6-round Carcano clips are available at low cost. Reloading is precluded by its special Berdan primer, and this cartridge is not produced in this country although cases can be formed from 6.5 mm. Mannlicher-Schoenauer cases.

Specifications
ITALIAN MODEL 38 CARCANO RIFLE
MECHANISM TYPE: Turnbolt; fixed box-magazine
CALIBER: 7.35 mm.
WEIGHT: 8.2 lbs.
BARREL LENGTH: 21.1"
OVER-ALL LENGTH: 40.0"
MAGAZINE CAPACITY: 6 rounds
SIGHTS: Inverted V front; open fixed rear
RIFLING: 4 grooves, right twist

Italian Model 38 Carcano Rifle. Between the World Wars the Italians experimented with rifles of larger caliber than their 6.5 mm., and in 1938 adopted a 7.35 mm. Carcano which was extensively used in World War II. Except for its turned-down bolt handle, the Model 38 Carcano has the same action as the Italian Model 1891 rifle and uses a similar cartridge clip. Unlike the Model 1891, it has uniform pitch rifling. It is a simple, sturdy arm, but lacks fine workmanship and finish.

Like the Model 1891 Carcano, this rifle is not well suited for sporter conversion. However, it is fairly light and compact, and a handy hunting arm as issued. Most specimens are in good to excellent condition.

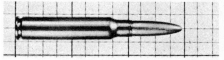

7.35 MM. CARCANO CARTRIDGE (BALL)
TYPE: Rimless, bottleneck case
BULLET: 128 grs.
POWDER: Chopped tube smokeless
MUZZLE VELOCITY: 2482 f.p.s.

7.35 mm. Carcano Cartridge. The 7.35 mm. Carcano is a necked-up version of the 6.5 mm. Model 91 Italian cartridge. Its rimless case has a large groove on the base encircling the primer, and markings are in relief and difficult to read. The semi-spitzer bullet has a steel jacket clad with gilding metal or cupronickel, and an aluminum filler in the forward part of the jacket makes the bullet long for its weight.

This cartridge is not produced in this country, but it is readily available in the original Italian military loading. It has a special-size Berdan primer not available in this country. A few bullet manufacturers sell soft-point 7.35 mm. bullets, and loading equipment and data are available. With the bullet and powder in the military cartridge replaced with a soft-point bullet and suitable charge, the 7.35 is satisfactory for deer hunting. Cases can be formed from 6.5 mm. Mannlicher-Schoenauer cases.

Italian Model 38 Carcano rifle

Austro-Hungarian Model 1895 Mannlicher rifle

Remington Model 1902 rifle

**Austro-Hungarian Model 1895 Mann-
licher Rifle.** The Austro-Hungarian
Model 1895 rifle was developed by
the Austrian arms designer, von Mannlicher, and adopted by Austria-Hungary
in 1895. It is of straight-pull type,
operated by moving the bolt straight
rearward and forward. A cam inside
the bolt turns the bolt head for
locking and unlocking. The single-column magazine requires a cartridge clip
for its operation. Operation is somewhat faster than a turnbolt rifle, but
not so reliable.

In addition to use by Austria-
Hungary, this rifle was employed by
Bulgaria, Greece, Yugoslavia, and
Romania. It was the standard Austro-
Hungarian rifle during World War I,
and many were captured by the Italians
and used by them in World War II.

This rifle was well made and finished,
but the condition of most specimens
leaves much to be desired. It is not
as plentiful in this country as several
other military rifles, and is not particularly suited for conversion to a sporter.

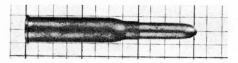

8x50R MANNLICHER CARTRIDGE (BALL)
TYPE: Rimmed, bottleneck case
BULLET: 244 grs.
POWDER: Flake smokeless
MUZZLE VELOCITY: 2034 f.p.s.

8x50R Mannlicher Cartridge. The
8x50R cartridge (cal. 8 mm. and
rimmed case 50 mm. long) has a relatively large body diameter and short
neck. It was introduced in 1888 as a
blackpowder round, but in 1890 a
smokeless powder loading was adopted.
The bullet is of round-nose type, and
has a lubricated steel jacket. Markings
include maker's initials, and month and
year of manufacture (Roman numeral
is used for the month). Italian-made
cartridge specimens are marked with
manufacturer's initials and last 3 digits
of the production year.

This cartridge is produced in Europe
and England, but not in this country.
Military ammunition in this caliber is
sold by a few dealers. Loading equipment is available, but not loading data
with current powders, and reloading
requires special Berdan primers and a
special decapping tool.

**Yugoslavian Model 95M Mannlicher
Rifle.** One of the many different rifles
adopted by Yugoslavia after World War
I was the Model 95M Mannlicher. This
rifle was converted from the 8 mm.
Austrian Model 95, and is similar to
the Greek Model 95/24 Mannlicher
rifle. The M following Model 95 is an
abbreviation for the word *modernized*.

Conversion from the Austrian Model
95 Mannlicher rifle included rebarreling
to cal. 8 mm. Mauser, modifying bolt
head and extractor, closing in magazine
bottom, providing clip slots on receiver
bridge, and fitting a tangent curve rear
sight and long handguard.

Yugoslavia used this rifle in World
War II. Many captured by Germans
were used by police and security forces.
It is well made and safe, but not as
reliable as most turnbolt rifles.

The 95M is better adapted for shooting than the Model 95 Austro-Hungarian Mannlicher because of the easy
availability of 8 mm. Mauser cartridges.
Considerable numbers of this rifle were
sold in this country, and most specimens
are in fair to good condition.

Remington Model 1902 Rifle. The
7 mm. Remington Model 1902 military
rifle was sold principally in Central and
South America. It has a single-shot rolling-block action resembling that of
Remington blackpowder rifles. The
original rolling-block action was pat-

ented by Leonard Geiger in 1863, and
Joseph Rider, a Remington employee,
improved it in 1864.

Not all 7 mm. rolling-block rifles are
suited for shooting. Many specimens
are badly rusted, especially the bores,
and show damaging effects of years in
a tropical climate. Furthermore, most
7 mm. military rolling-block rifles *have
excessive headspace for modern 7 mm.
ammunition.*

Apparently these rifles are adapted
to a 7 mm. Mauser cartridge with longer head-to-shoulder dimensions than the
7 mm. sporting cartridge standardized
by the Sporting Arms & Ammunition
Manufacturers' Institute about 1920.

7 MM. MAUSER CARTRIDGE (BALL)
TYPE: Rimless, bottleneck case
BULLET: 173 grs.
POWDER: Flake smokeless
MUZZLE VELOCITY: 2296 f.p.s.

7 mm. Mauser Cartridge. The 7 mm.
Mauser cartridge was first introduced
in 1892 with an early type of the Spanish Mauser. It is a widely used military
cartridge, especially in Central and
South America, and also a well-known
and popular round for sporting rifles.

The 7 mm. Mauser cartridge is produced in this country and many others,
in a variety of military and sporting
loads. The 7 mm. German-made military round shown has a round-nose
bullet with cupronickel-clad steel jacket,
and is marked D. M. (German Metallic
Cartridge Co.), K. for Karlsruhe to denote place of manufacture, and numbers to show month and year of production.

This cartridge is produced in this
country and imported in a variety of
sporting loads which are excellent for
big-game hunting. Loading data, equipment, and components for this caliber
are readily available. ∎

Yugoslavian Model 95M Mannlicher rifle

Some Interesting Clips

By Charles H. Yust, Jr.

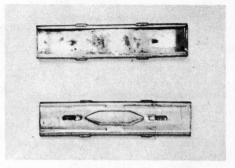

ARGENTINA—Clip for any model 7.65 mm. Argentine Mauser rifle from Model 1891 on. Holds 5 cartridges. Made of plated or tinned brass with steel spring

AUSTRIA—Clip for Austrian 11.15 x 58R mm. blackpowder repeating rifle Model 1885, the first Mannlicher clip-loading rifle. Holds 5 cartridges. Loaded steel clip is inserted into top of magazine in only one way. As last cartridge case is ejected, lower angle-arm of clip-ejector lever flips empty clip out through top of receiver, the bottom being closed

AUSTRIA—Clip for Austrian 11.15 x 58R mm. blackpowder repeating rifle Model 1886. Holds 5 cartridges. Loaded clip, stamped in rhomboid form from sheet steel, is inserted into magazine from top in only one way. A catch at rear of magazine body snaps into clip and holds it in place. Empty clip falls through narrow opening in bottom of magazine, the first Mannlicher clip to be so ejected. Loose cartridges cannot be placed in magazine, and clip is essential part of magazine

THERE are many phases of arms study which have yet to become popular. I would like to point out the study of clips which has been largely overlooked, but has proved very interesting.

This article is based on notes gathered over some years, citing specimens of clips in my collection and the collections of friends. It sets forth some of the available unusual, rare, not so rare, and more commonplace types.

Because they are so well known, United States clips have not been included with one exception. That is the clip for the .276 cal. Pedersen semi-automatic rifle. None of the other experimental clips was available.

With the exception of clips for the British .276 Pattern 1913 experimental rifle, and the Argentine and Mexican Mauser, none of the conventional flat Mauser-type clips has been included. The famous Mannlicher series is almost completely covered, also the British series, French, Italian, Imperial and Soviet Russian, and Swiss.

The rare clips are the Austrian Model 1885 and Model 1886; the British .276 Pattern 1913; British .276 Pedersen semi-automatic rifle; French Model 1917 St. Etienne semi-automatic rifle; French Daudeteau rifle; United States .276 Pedersen semi-automatic rifle; the Dormus, Bittner, and Bergmann pistols.

I do not mean to imply that these are out of reach of the collector. Except for the Bergmann, I have seen all the clips included in this article, and all but about 8 are in my own collection.

Clips and chargers defined

The British divide clips into 2 groups, termed 'clips' and 'chargers'.

The British *Textbook of Small Arms, 1909*, discussed this subject as follows:

"Cartridges are carried in chargers and clips in order to accelerate the rapid loading of the magazine. Chargers are used by being placed in grooves (clip guides) in the body over the magazine,

CHARLES H. YUST, JR., of Hudson, Ohio, has been a student of arms for nearly 40 years. He is author of numerous articles on guns and ammunition.

where the cartridges are swept out of them by the thumb into the magazine, and the empty charger thrown away."

Clips with their cartridges are placed in the magazine, the clip being held down by a catch, as in Mannlicher types from the Austrian Model 1886 on. The cartridges are fed up by the magazine lever, or platform, which is made sufficiently narrow to pass between the sides of the clip. When the cartridges are expended the clip falls out through an opening in the bottom of the magazine.

Chargers are usually made of steel. When used with rimless cartridges, their sides do not extend much past the extractor groove around the base of the cartridge. In this type of charger, known as the Mauser, a thin undulating flat spring presses the cartridges forward, so that the extractor grooves bear firmly against the ribs on each side of the charger which act as guides to the extractor grooves.

Rimmed cartridges require more support to prevent their getting askew while being pressed down into the magazine. Thus the sides of the Russian and British chargers extend further along the cartridges, to keep them in line by lateral pressure.

The Swiss charger consists of a millboard receptacle open at the bottom.

The Dutch and Romanian clips are very similar. Their backs are slightly curved because of the cartridge rims being so much larger than the bodies. The sides of the clips at each end are turned slightly inward to retain the cartridges.

The Italian Mannlicher clip, being for rimless cartridges, has a straight back, as the cartridges lie practically parallel.

The United States gives the standard name 'clip' to this item regardless of the manner in which it is used, while, as has been noted, the British use the 2 terms 'clip' and 'charger'. This could be confusing. To circumvent this problem, I employ the United States system and use the term 'clip'. However, where an official nomenclature is known, it is included.

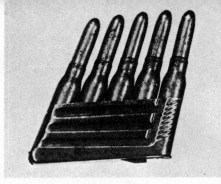

AUSTRIA—Model 1888 clip for Austrian 8 x 50R mm. repeating rifle Model 1888 and Model 1888/90. Holds 5 cartridges. Clip is scaled-down Model 1886 type, and function and operation of magazine and clip in Models 1888 and 1888/90 are same as in Model 1886. Model 1888 was the first modern small caliber repeating rifle employed in warfare (Chilean Civil War of 1891). This arm was also adopted by Bulgaria and Greece. Clip may also be used in all arms in which Model 1890 clip is used (see below)

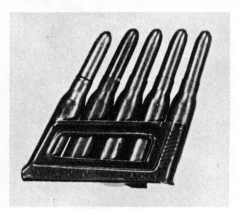

AUSTRIA—Austrian Mannlicher Model 1890 clip is usable in Austrian Mannlicher 8 x 50R mm. rifles from Model 1888 through Model 1890, Model 1895, Model 1930 conversion of Model 1895, and Hungarian Model 1935. Holds 5 cartridges. Clips of Austrian and Hungarian manufacture are generally made of blued steel. Captured Austrian Model 1895 rifles and carbines were used by Italian Army in World War II and cartridges and clips for these arms were manufactured in Italian arsenals. Italian clips are of blued steel, brass, and cadmium-plated steel. Other materials or coatings may have been used. Bulgaria, China, Czechoslovakia, Ethiopia, Greece, Poland, and Yugoslavia also adopted or used this weapon

AUSTRIA — Clip for Model 1894 Dormus 8 mm. automatic pistol. Holds 5 cartridges. Formed of sheet steel, clip is loaded through top of pistol, with breechblock open, into fixed magazine in butt, a feature similar to that of early Mannlicher pistols. Clip formed part of action, in same manner as Mannlicher rifle clips, and could be

inserted into magazine only one way. This weapon, made in small quantities in Austria to design of a Maj. Dormus, was of straight blowback design

AUSTRIA — Clip for Bittner 7.65 mm. repeating pistol, formed of sheet steel, patented by Gustav Bittner of Weipert, Bohemia (Austria), about 1893. (Weapon was not semi-automatic but was a manually-operated magazine repeating pistol.) Holds 5 cartridges. Formed of sheet steel, clip can be inserted into magazine only one way, and operates like Austrian Mannlicher rifles of the 1886 to 1895 Models. When new clip is pressed into magazine from above, empty clip is forced out bottom

FRANCE—Clip Model 1890 for 3-shot magazine series of Berthier rifles and carbines, such as carbines Model 1890, 1892, and later modifications, as well as rifles Indo-China Model 1902, Colonial Model 1907, and standard Model 1907/15, all chambered for 8 mm. Lebel. Made of blued steel, clip can be inserted into magazine either end down and functions in the same manner as Austrian, Netherlands, and Romanian clips

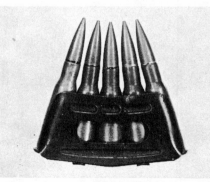

FRANCE—Clip Model 1916, First Type, for 1916 modification (addition of magazine extension) of Berthier rifle and carbine, and Model 1918 St. Etienne semi-automatic rifle, all chambered for 8 mm. Lebel. Holds 5 cartridges. Made of blued steel, clip has 2 magazine catch projections on base instead of only 1 as in Model 1890. Upper rib on clip is divided into 3 sections

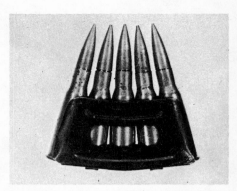

FRANCE—Clip Model 1916, Second Type. Identical with First Type, except that upper rib is unbroken

FRANCE—Clip Model 1917 for use in Model 1917 St. Etienne semi-automatic rifle using 8 mm. Lebel cartridge. Holds 5 cartridges. Made of blued steel, clip can be inserted into magazine either end down. This clip will not function in Model 1916 Berthier weapons, nor will Model 1916 clip function in Model 1917 St. Etienne weapon. One reason for introduction of Model 1918 St. Etienne semi-automatic rifle was so that Model 1916 Berthier clips could be used. Rare collector's item

FRANCE—Clip for Daudeteau 6.5 mm. rimmed rifle and carbine, a French Model 1895 naval arm. Holds 5 No. 12 Daudeteau cartridges. Made of blued steel, clip has red stripe painted along left end as guide in loading, as clip can be used only one way. Design principle is like that of Swiss Schmidt-Rubin clip, although material is different. Right end of clip is open while flaps at bottom and large flap at neck of cartridges project inward to prevent rounds falling out. Broad opening for thumb is cut partly down one side and completely down other side to enable cartridges to be swept into magazine. When bolt is closed, clip is flipped aside. Daudeteau rifle and carbine were used by Uruguay also. These weapons, cartridges, and clips are very rare

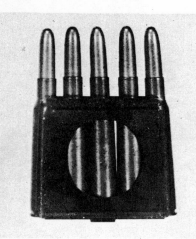

GERMANY—Clip introduced with German 7.92 x 57 mm. repeating rifle Model 1888. Holds 5 cartridges. Clip may be inserted either end down, and functions within magazine like Austrian Models 1886 to 1895, Netherlands, and Romanian clips. Made of brass, blued steel, and an almost clear lacquered steel, clip is also used in Mannlicher Model 1904 rifle and Mannlicher Model 1891 semi-automatic experimental rifle

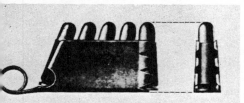

GERMANY—Clip for Bergmann 5 mm. No. 2 semi-automatic pistol, Model 1894. Holds 5 cartridges. Clip is formed of sheet steel. Though used in same general manner as Mannlicher rifle clips, clip could be removed through bottom of magazine before shooting and magazine could be loaded with loose cartridges

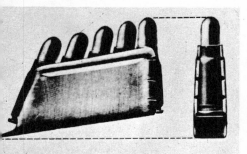

GERMANY—Clip for Bergmann 6.5 mm. No. 3 semi-automatic pistol, Model 1894. Holds 5 cartridges. Formed of sheet steel, clip used in same manner as 5 mm. clip

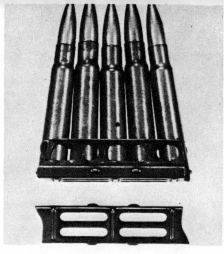

GREAT BRITAIN—Mark II clip (Charger, .303" Cartridge, Mark II) holds 5 cartridges. Made of blued steel, clip has spring stop at each end to prevent cartridges falling out and is strengthened by 3 ridges on base. A Roman numeral II is stamped into side. Mark II clip superseded Mark I clip (Charger, .303" Cartridge, Mark I/C—not illustrated) introduced with Rifle, Short, Magazine, Lee-Enfield. Mark I clip lacks 3 strengthening ridges on base, or spring stop at each end

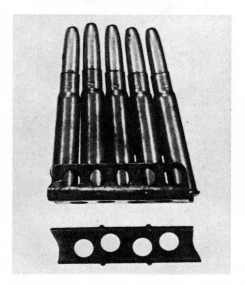

GREAT BRITAIN—Mark III clip (Charger .303" Cartridge, Mark III) holds 5 cartridges. Made of blued steel, Mark III clip has openwork design different from that of first 2 Marks. Clip base is altered and there are 5 openings in side, including left opening which in all these .303" clips is split to make the spring stop

GREAT BRITAIN—Mark IV clip (Charger, .303" Cartridge, Mark IV), made of blued steel, is almost identical with Mark III, except for only 4 openings in side

GREAT BRITAIN—Modified form of Mark IV clip with 4 openings in side walls. Mark number will usually be found stamped on side walls in Roman numerals, and there may also be a letter, which is manufacturer's symbol

GREAT BRITAIN—Pattern 1913 clip for British Enfield .276 experimental rifle. These clips differ from regular British design and are of flat pattern. Clip holds 5 cartridges, and is used in same manner as Lee-Enfield and Mauser clips. Body is steel, blackened, probably by a lacquer. Photographs show clip loaded as well as empty, top, bottom, and side views. Few of these rifles were manufactured, hence cartridges and clips are rare items

GREAT BRITAIN—Clip for .276 Pedersen experimental semi-automatic rifle. Holds 10 cartridges. Made of steel, tinned or cadmium-plated, clip can be inserted into magazine either end down. This clip was used in one variety of .276 Pedersen semi-automatic rifle manufactured in England for British trials. Though the Pedersen rifle underwent extensive experimentation in the United States from 1924 to 1932, this clip is not interchangeable with U. S. Pedersen clip as magazines are different in shape, although rest of rifles are apparently identical and chambered for same cartridge

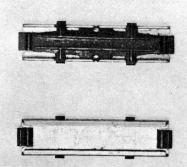

GREECE—Clip for 6.5 x 53 mm. Mannlicher-Schoenauer service rifle and carbines Model 1903 and Model 1903/14. Holds 5 cartridges. Body of clip is almost identical with flat Mauser type, but spring arrangement differs. Body of clip is made of bright steel with spring of blued steel. Clip is flipped from clip guide when bolt is closed

ITALY—Clip for Vetterli-Vitali 10.4 mm. Model 1871/87 rifle and carbine. Holds 4 cartridges. Made of wood, spring steel, and cord, clip is set over magazine opening and forced straight down into magazine. Then knotted cord is grasped between thumb and finger and pulled straight upward to strip cartridges from clip into magazine

ITALY—Clip for Model 1891 6.5 mm. Mannlicher-Carcano rifle and carbine employing Mannlicher-type magazine. Holds 6 cartridges. Made of brass and tinned, blued, Parkerized, and cadmium-plated steel, clip is held in magazine until last round is used, and then pushed out bottom of magazine when new clip is forced in from top. Clip was also used with Vetterli rifles and carbines altered during World War I to 6.5 mm. Mannlicher-Carcano caliber and equipped with Mannlicher-type magazine. In 1938, when Italy increased caliber of rifle and carbine to 7.35 mm., same magazine and clip were retained

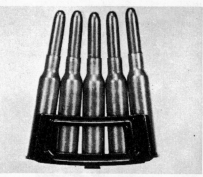

NETHERLANDS—Clip for Netherlands Mannlicher 6.5 x 53R mm. rifle Model 1895. Holds 5 cartridges and is made of steel and lacquered black. Clip can be inserted into magazine either end down and functions same as in Austrian Mannlicher rifles Models 1886 to 1895. Netherlands and Romanian Mannlicher clips are interchangeable. Commercial clip of tinned steel with openings in side wall slightly larger than in Netherlands service clip is also encountered

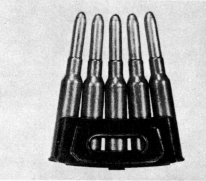

ROMANIA—Clip for Romanian 6.5 x 53R (Mannlicher) repeating rifles Model 1892 and Model 1893, and carbine Model 1893. Holds 5 cartridges. Made of blued steel, clip has same general shape as Netherlands service and commercial version, except cutout in side walls is smaller and different in shape. Function of clip in magazine is identical with that of the Netherlands, and is interchangeable

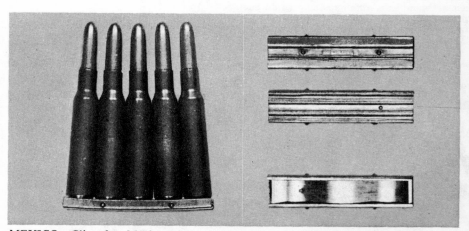

MEXICO—Clips for Mexican 7 mm. Mauser rifles. Holds 5 cartridges. Clips are familiar Mauser pattern. Two styles have been encountered, as illustrated. Upper clip at right has tinned brass body with steel spring and name "MEXICO" stamped on bottom. Lower clip differs in bottom of body, which has 3 longitudinal grooves, has only one spring locking stud, is made of untinned brass, and name is not stamped on it

RUSSIA—Imperial Russian Model 1891 clip for use in 7.62 mm. "3-Line" Nagant rifles and carbines. Holds 5 cartridges. Made of bright stamped steel, formed with solid high side walls, clip is shaped like British clips minus side walls and bottom perforations. Made of much lighter gauge metal. Clip has flap at each end of both side walls bent slightly inward to retain 5 cartridges. Identifying trademarks or initials of manufacturers in United States, England, Germany, Austria, and other nations may be found on bottom

RUSSIA—Soviet clip, date of introduction unknown, for use in all "3-Line" Nagant rifles and carbines. Clip is identical with Model 1891 except side walls are not quite so high and have no cutout flaps at ends. Cartridges are held in clip by upper end portions of side walls forced slightly inward. Used in same manner as British clip, it can be inserted either end down

SWITZERLAND—Clip of earlier Swiss pattern. The millboard may be of more than one color, depending on type of cartridge loaded in clip. Dark brown is for ball, violet for armor-piercing, white for blank (another blank uses a green clip), red for drill rounds (dummy). Clip can be inserted into clip guide only one way

SWITZERLAND—Clip for Swiss 7.5 mm. Schmidt-Rubin service rifles and carbines from 1889 to 1931. It can be used in Mannlicher Model 1893 carbine, but not in single-shot Cadet rifle. Holds 6 cartridges. Clip consists of a millboard receptacle open at bottom. Bottom edges of sides and ends are formed of tin. Four flaps, which project inward, retain cartridges. A broad thumb groove is cut partly down one side, and completely down other side

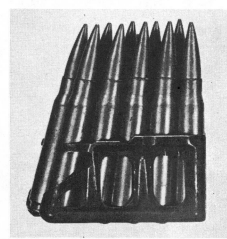

UNITED STATES—Clip for .276 Pedersen semi-automatic rifle T1, experimented with from 1924 until 1932. Holds 10 cartridges. Made of steel, clip can be inserted into gun only with slanted end down. Clip remains in magazine until last round is fired, and is then expelled from top of action. Clip has many perforations along with strengthening ribs on sides and bottom. Weapon and clip are real collector's items today ■

A MAN TO REMEMBER

A. A. CHASSEPOT

Invented the Chassepot
needlegun

Born—Mutzig, France, 1833
Died—Paris, 1905

ANTOINE ALPHONSE CHASSEPOT was born and reared as a gunmaker. His father was an armorer at Mutzig, and the younger Chassepot early decided to follow his father's profession. At 23 he was sufficiently skilled to obtain work in the government arms factory at Mutzig, where he made such an outstanding record that he was transferred to the central arms plant in Paris within 2 years. There he quickly became director of the factory and Controller of Arms for the nation.

It was while he was working in Paris that Chassepot began his experimentation in rifle design. In 1863 he invented his first breech-loading percussion rifle. It was a good arm, but never became popular, probably because the percussion system was on the way out. Three years later, in 1866, he developed his famous breech-loading bolt-action needlegun which took a center-primed paper cartridge. The new rifle was an immediate success, being adopted by the French Army as the Model 1866. It was the first breech-loader used by the French Army, and the system was adopted for carbines and musketoons as well as for rifles. In 1874 it was modified by Gras to take a metallic cartridge, and continued in use until supplanted by the Lebel in 1886. The Saxon Army also adopted the system in 1873 (captured arms from Franco-Prussian War converted to handle 11 mm. Mauser cartridge).

For his invention Chassepot received the cross of the Legion of Honor in 1866. He remained at his job in the arms factory but seems to have ceased his experimental work and gradually drifted into obscurity until his death at the age of 72.— HAROLD L. PETERSON

PROOF MARKS

PROOF of a firearm has been defined as the "testing of a new small arm before sale to insure so far as practicable its safety in the hands of its user".

Proving of a firearm, as a test of safety, is done by firing a proof load developing higher pressure than that of the load normally used so there will be a margin of strength in the arm and, consequently, a measure of safety for the user.

Upon satisfactory completion of proof firing, the arm is usually stamped with proof marks signifying that the arm has satisfactorily withstood the strain of proof pressure without perceptible or measurable change in the condition of the arm.

Origin of proof marks

It is difficult to determine when proof marks were first employed on firearms, but there is evidence that they were used in Europe as early as the 16th century, when gun barrels were proved and stamped by guild officials or city authorities. Many so-called proof marks on early firearms are in reality special gunmaker's symbols or inspection stamps, and there is still much researching required to determine the true significance of many early markings.

In course of time, proof of firearms became systematized, and was performed by national governments in most European arms-producing countries. Each of these nations established its own proof house, proof procedures and marks, and passed laws requiring that firearms be subjected to government proof before sale and use. This was beneficial to both firearms users and reputable gunmakers, and has endured in many countries to the present.

Proof in various nations

In this country, firearms proof is not required except for military arms, and there is no national proof house. The government has its own system of proof testing and proof marks for military arms, and each commercial manufacturer conducts tests which he deems proper. Although proof testing is not required, the established U. S. manufacturers are careful to protect their reputations by turning out soundly-made guns. The majority have their own distinctive marks consisting of letters or various symbols. Some of these marks are not proof marks, but merely manufacturer's symbols.

There have been many attempts, especially on the part of European countries, for international standardization of proof tests, but this has never been achieved. Consequently, each country requiring firearms proof has its own system of tests and markings, but most nations recognize proof marks of other countries. Proof tests and marks for military arms are usually different from those for commercial guns. Authentic information on military proof marks is generally much more difficult to obtain than data on proof marks employed on commercial arms.

Types of proof marks

Proof marks are stamped on the barrel, action components, or stock, but most usually on barrel, receiver, or frame. In some cases the gun must be disassembled to find them. There is a great variety of these marks, each with its special meaning. Some of them, such as inspection or view marks, and figures to denote caliber, gauge, case length, bullet weight, and other specifications,

---

GREAT BRITAIN

London   **Birmingham**

Provisional proof for barrels

NOT NITRO   BLACK POWDER

Definitive proof with blackpowder

Definitive proof with smokeless powder

BELGIUM

Provisional blackpowder proof (at present obligatory for smoothbore breech-loading guns, and voluntary for guns with rifled barrels)

Definitive blackpowder proof for smoothbore breech-loading guns; also indicates proof of small-bore guns and handguns

Acceptance or inspection mark following definitive proof, commonly called the "tower mark"

Smokeless powder proof

FRANCE

Paris   **St. Etienne**

Provisional proof of barrels in the rough

Ordinary proof of barrels finished except for polishing

Ordinary blackpowder proof of completed arms

Ordinary smokeless powder proof with "T" powder

GERMANY
pre-World War II

Provisional proof

Second proof with inspection stamp

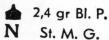
2,4 gr Bl. P.
St. M. G.

Smokeless proof for rifles with charge weight (2.4 grams flake powder), and use of steel-jacketed bullet (St.M.G.)

Germany and Austria (1939-45) | West Germany

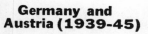

Provisional proof of shotguns and multi-barrel guns

Definitive blackpowder proof

Definitive smokeless powder proof

AUSTRIA
Vienna | Ferlach

Provisional proof of barrels for shotguns and multi-barrel guns

Definitive blackpowder proof

Definitive smokeless powder proof

ITALY

Provisional proof ot Brescia Proof House

Provisional proof of Gardone Proof House

PN

Definitive proof with blackpowder

PSF

Definitive proof with smokeless powder

FINITO

Proof after assembly of gun

SPAIN

Mark of Eibar Proof House

Obligatory blackpowder proof of smooth-bore breech-loading guns

F E

Manufacture within established tolerances

are not proof marks in the true sense, but are usually classified as such. Countries change their proof laws and procedures from time to time, and thus in attempting to learn the significance of proof marks on a gun it is necessary to refer to a list of marks which were used when the gun was manufactured.

Typical proof of a commercial European gun consists of a first or 'provisional' proof of the barrel in its unfinished state followed by a final or 'definitive' proof of complete gun when finished or almost finished. There is also a 'nitro' proof to indicate test with smokeless powder, voluntary proof of arms not ordinarily subject to proof, proof after repair, proof of guns imported into a country, and special proofs for rimfire arms, signal pistols, and other types of arms. Each of these has its special proof mark which is part of an extremely complex heraldry. Sometimes rules of proof and proof marks were not strictly followed, and many arms lack the required marks, or have unknown marks not conforming to proof rules. Sometimes spurious proof marks are used.

Significance of proof marks

In order to clarify the significance of proof marks, the Guardians of the Birmingham Proof House in England issued in 1953, and reprinted in 1958, a memorandum entitled "Limitation in the Proof of Small Arms", in which these comments are made:

"Perhaps because of the confidence created by the Proof Marks impressed on arms made in this country a confused idea appears to have grown up that the British Proof Marks are in fact a hall mark of quality. . . .

"Proof is solely a test of the ability of a small arm to withstand the pressures and strains imposed on its parts by normal service use—and particularly the pressure developed by the propellant gases of the cartridge or load for which the arm is designed. . . .

"Proof may therefore be described as a test of safety, but it is not a test of quality because the Proof Test is uniform for all arms of the same bore having the same chamber length . . . and each may qualify to be marked according to the Rules of Proof.

"It is part of the duty of the Proof Authorities to determine what is in fit condition for Proof and whether arms have passed or failed Proof but they are not the arbiters of what is fit for sale."

The proof marks illustrated are representative of many important ones. Some shown are obsolete, but are often encountered on arms of older manufacture. ∎

Questions and Answers

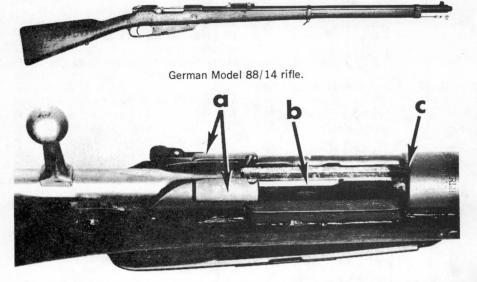

German Model 88/14 rifle.

Three principal modifications are: (a) clip-slot plates on receiver bridge, (b) cartridge retaining rib in left wall of receiver and (c) rounded cut on rear of receiver to clear bullet noses during loading.

Modified Model 1888 Rifle

I recently encountered a German Model 1888 cal. 8 mm. military rifle which appears to have been modified for use with Mauser-type strip clips. On top of the receiver bridge are two steel plates each with a clip slot. The left wall of the receiver is slotted for a spring-loaded rib which retains the cartridges in the magazine, and the top left side of the receiver has a circular cut to provide clearance for the thumb during loading. It appears that the clip-slot plates are welded or brazed to the receiver. The opening in the magazine bottom is closed by a sheet steel plate. Were these modifications official?

Answer: The modifications were official, and the modified rifle was designated Model 88/14. In addition to the modifications you mention, there are the following:

1. A rounded cut on the upper rear of the receiver ring to provide clearance for bullet noses when loading the magazine.
2. Diameter of chamber neck and bullet seat enlarged to permit use of the 8 mm. (7.9 mm.) S-type cartridge with .323″ diameter pointed bullet. The receiver ring is marked "S" to denote this modification.
3. Clip latch removed from trigger guard-magazine assembly, and filler plates inserted.
4. Short leaf of rear sight removed, elevation markings on large leaf milled away, and new markings for S cartridge stamped on.

Because of these modifications, Model 88/14 rifles used the same cartridge and clip as the Model 98 Mauser which replaced the Model 1888 as the standard German shoulder arm. This standardization of ammunition and loading procedure was a big advantage, especially during World War I.

According to the book *Die Handwaffen des brandenburgisch-preussisch-deutschen Heeres* by Eckardt-Morawietz, there were two other modified Model 1888 rifles, the 88/05 and 88S. Modifications on the Model 88/05 are generally similar to those of the Model 88/14, but the clip-slot plates of the 88/05 are fastened to the receiver with screws instead of by brazing, and the large rear sight leaf calibrated for the S cartridge is of new manufacture. Eckardt-Morawietz stated that 370,000 Model 1888 rifles were converted to Model 88/05.

Modifications on the Model 88S are not very extensive. The magazine is unaltered, and this rifle is used with the Mannlicher-type packet clip which is loaded into the magazine with the cartridges. The chamber neck and bullet seat, as well as the rear sight, are modified for the S cartridge.

Most German Model 1888 rifles encountered in the U.S. have only the chamber neck and bullet seat modified for the S cartridge. Eckardt-Morawietz stated that the bores of many specimens were also

Modified rear sight (l.) of Model 88/14 rifle in comparison with unmodified rear sight of Model 1888 rifle.

modified by deepening the grooves to give a groove diameter of 8.2 mm. (.3228″). This measurement corresponds closely to the .323″ diameter of the S bullet.

A Model 88/14 rifle examined by *The American Rifleman* Technical Staff has the chamber neck and bullet seat modified for the S bullet, but the groove diameter is .319″ to fit the .318″ diameter of the Model 1888 round-nose bullet. In firing an S cartridge in this bore, the bullet diameter would be reduced .004″. While this is not ideal, the bearing surface of the S bullet is extremely short, and evidently the S cartridge gave acceptable results with the .319″ groove diameter.

Despite the modified chamber neck and bullet seat, it is not advisable to fire an S cartridge in a Model 1888 rifle or its modified variants.— L.O.

Threaded shank of Mauser 98 barrel.

Mauser 98 Barrel Threads

I want to fit a replacement barrel on a German Mauser 98 military action which has a large-diameter receiver ring, and need information on specifications of the threads. It appears that the V threads of the old barrel I removed from the receiver are 60° included angle, and a friend tells me that there are 12 and a fraction threads per inch. Can you furnish the information?

Answer: The V threads on Mauser 98 barrels are of British Whitworth form with a rounded crest and root, and the included angle is 55°, not 60°.

Threads on three German Mauser 98 military barrels were measured with an optical comparator by *The American Rifleman* Technical Staff. Two of these barrels were from Model 98 infantry rifles of World War I, and the other was from a carbine 98k barrel produced during World War II. All three barrels have 12 threads per inch, and the diameter over the threaded portion is 1.10″

Many Mauser 98 replacement barrels produced in the U.S. have threads with 60° included angle. While these barrels are not an ideal fit, they are generally serviceable. Such barrels, when screwed part way into the receiver, can usually be moved from side to side somewhat since the threads are not mated perfectly with those in the receiver. There is almost no sideward movement with Mauser 98 issue barrels and others having proper-fitting 55° threads.—L.O.